# WRITE ALL ABOUT IT

# WRITE ALL ABOUT IT

by Andrea Leis and Robert Chodos

**New Readers Press**
*Publishing Division of Laubach Literacy International*
Syracuse, New York

## About the Authors

Andrea Leis teaches adults. From her experience teaching high school equivalency (GED) preparation, adult basic education, and English-as-a-second-language in school, prison, and factory settings, she became aware of the need for an English workbook for adults that emphasized writing instead of grammar. She consulted with her husband, writer Robert Chodos, who had first learned news style on his college newspaper and has since applied it to various forms of writing and to teaching English.

Together they devised *Write All About It,* based on newspaper style and content. It is their hope that the workbook's adult orientation and journalistic approach to writing will ease writer's cramp and promote clearer expression.

The authors have two children, Sarah and David, and live in New Hamburg, Ontario. At the time this book was written, however, they lived in Clinton, Massachusetts.

Although Clinton is used as the name of a community in this book, all news stories, letters, and examples and the characters mentioned in them are completely fictitious.

ISBN 0-88336-375-5     STUDENT'S EDITION

© 1986

EACH ONE TEACH ONE

New Readers Press
Publishing Division of Laubach Literacy International
Box 131, Syracuse, New York 13210

Printed in the United States of America

Edited by Kay Koschnick
Designed by Chris Steenwerth
Cover by Chris Steenwerth

9 8 7 6 5 4 3

## Note to Students

The goal of this workbook is to teach writing skills using newspaper style. When we learn how to talk, we do not necessarily learn how to make a point. Similarly, we may learn grammar but not how to write. The emphasis in this book is on learning how to write clearly.

Newswriting has its own style. Many people read newspapers even if they don't read books. Because the purpose of newspapers is to provide information, newswriting must be clear and concise. People often don't take the time to read whole stories carefully, so newswriters have to convey information quickly and accurately. The style they use encourages a maximum of information in a minimum of space.

Even if you don't plan on writing for a newspaper, the basic ideas of newspaper style can be applied to all forms of writing. The skills you learn from newspaper style will help you make yourself understood whether you are leaving a note for your friend, applying for a job, or writing a memo to your boss.

# Table of Contents

# — Part 1 —

# Sentences

In the first three chapters of this book, we will look at some basic things about sentences:

— how to tell the difference between complete and incomplete sentences
— how to use capital letters in sentences
— how to mark the end of a sentence with the correct punctuation.

# 1. Complete Sentences

## Subject and Verb

A complete sentence expresses a complete thought. It has a subject (someone or something) and a verb (the action). In the following sentences, the subject is underlined once, and the verb is underlined twice:

> Mary wore her coat.

> Rain soaked the ground.

The subject may not always be the first part of a sentence. To find the subject and verb, first ask yourself, "What is the action?" That is the verb. Then ask, "Who or what did it?" That is the subject.

> Farther south, people swim in October.

> Last week, all the snow melted.

**Linking verbs.** The verb is not always active. There are also linking verbs and passive verbs. The most common linking verb is the verb *be*. It takes many different forms: *am, is, are, was, were, will be, would be, has been, have been.*

> For warmth, a fur coat is the best thing.

> Last Tuesday was a foggy day.

> This winter has been the coldest one in many years.

**Helping verbs in verb phrases.** Note that in the third sentence the verb is made up of two words: the helping verb *has* and the main verb *been*. It is very common for a verb to be made up of a main verb and one or more helping verbs. Such a verb is called a verb phrase.

> The wind is blowing hard today.

Here, *blowing* is the main verb and *is* is the helping verb.

The most common helping verbs are forms of the verb *be*. Other common helping verbs are *has, have, do, does, did, can, may, might, must, shall, will, could, would, should.*

> The snowplow will be coming this afternoon.

> We should have been working today.

**Passive verbs.** When the verb is passive, the action is something that happens to the subject.

> The <u>snow</u> <u>was removed</u> by the town roads department.
>
> The <u>sun</u> <u>is hidden</u> by the clouds.

**Verbs in questions.** To find the subject and the verb in a question, change the order of the words so that it reads like a statement.

> (Question)    Should I wear my boots today?
> (Statement)   I should wear my boots today.
>                        Subject: <u>I</u>    Verb: <u>should wear</u>
>
> (Question)    Did she go out without her hat?
> (Statement)   She did go out without her hat.
>                        Subject: <u>she</u>    Verb: <u>did go</u>

**Imperative verbs.** A command like *Open the door* expresses a complete thought. *Open* is the verb. But what is the subject? In sentences that give commands, the subject is the person who is being spoken to. A sentence that gives a command is called an imperative sentence. The subject of an imperative sentence is referred to as "you understood."

> Button up your overcoat.
> Subject: <u>you</u> understood    Verb: <u>button</u>
>
> Please shovel the driveway and the walk.
> Subject: <u>you</u> understood    Verb: <u>shovel</u>

**Assignment:** In Stories 1 and 2, underline the subject once and the verb twice in each sentence. Insert and underline the word *you* in imperative sentences. The first sentence is done for you.

### Story 1

Heavy <u>snow</u> <u>blanketed</u> Clinton yesterday for the second time this winter.

Snow plows were out before dawn this morning. Much snow still remained on Clinton's streets, however.

Clinton police issued guidelines for motorists. They were:

— Avoid unnecessary travel.

— Drive slowly.

— Park only in private driveways.

Is my trip necessary? Every motorist should ask that question, according to Clinton police.

### Story 2

When will the heat end? Many Clintonians are asking this question. For the sixth day in a row, people sweltered in the blistering summer heat today.

Wading pools were out in many backyards. Town residents flocked to nearby state parks.

The Todd County Board of Health still considers the town beach unsafe for swimming, however. Stay away from the beach. The board issued this warning again this morning.

The board closed the beach last Monday because of a high bacteria count in the water. The bacteria count yesterday was lower than Monday's count. It was still not low enough for safe swimming, however, according to the board.

Local stores reported a run on air conditioners and fans. Sales of bathing suits were also brisk.

# Compound Subjects and Verbs

A sentence can have one subject and two or more verbs. Likewise, a sentence can have two or more subjects and just one verb.

**Compound subjects.** Two or more subjects with the same verb are called a compound subject. The subjects are connected by a joining word. The most common joining words are *and* and *or*.

The following sentences have compound subjects:

Monday and Tuesday will be colder.

Rain, snow, and sleet fell yesterday.

Rain or hail is expected tomorrow also.

Sometimes the subject is followed by an *of* phrase. This can trick you into thinking that the word after *of* is the subject. It isn't.

Miles and miles of farmland were flooded.

**Compound verbs.** Two or more verbs with the same subject are called a compound verb. The verbs are connected by a joining word. The most common joining words are *and, or*, and *but*.

The following sentences have compound verbs:

The rivers rose and overflowed their banks.

Low bridges were covered with water or were destroyed.

A tornado was predicted but did not arrive.

**Assignment:** In Story 3, every sentence has a compound subject or a compound verb. Underline each subject once and each verb twice. The first sentence is done for you.

## Story 3

Fishermen, boaters, and golfers in the Clinton area can expect a perfect weekend. Saturday and Sunday will be mostly clear and sunny, according to the National Weather Service. Temperatures will reach 80 to 85 in the daytime but will fall to lows of 50 to 55 at night.

Meanwhile, in the West, inches and inches of rain are still falling. Thunderstorms started Thursday in Wyoming and are slowly moving eastward. Heavy rain and high winds knocked out power in Wyoming, Montana, and the Dakotas.

Floods left at least four people missing, closed roads, and forced people to leave their homes. In Cheyenne, Wyo., cars and trucks were swept away by the flow of water six feet deep in city streets.

# Sentence Fragments

**Subject or verb missing.** A sentence fragment does not express a complete thought. It does not have a subject and a verb. Sentence fragments are to be avoided in writing.

**Example 1:**     (Sentence fragment)
                   At noon on Wednesday.

This is not a complete thought. It does not tell us *what happened* at noon on Wednesday, and it does not tell us *who* or *what did it*. As written below, the sentence does tell these things.

                   (Complete sentence)
                   At noon on Wednesday, an accident occurred.

**Example 2:**     (Sentence fragment)
                   The man driving the green car.

This is not a complete thought. It does not tell us *what* the man driving the green car *did*. As written below, the sentence does tell this.

                   (Complete sentence)
                   The man driving the green car went through a stop sign.

**Dependent clauses.** The next example is a special kind of sentence fragment called a dependent clause. It contains a subject (*he*) and a verb (*had been*), but it is not a complete thought.

**Example 1:**     (Sentence fragment)
                   If he had been more careful.

This dependent clause does not tell us what would have happened if he had been more careful. A dependent clause depends on a main clause to make the thought complete. As written below, the sentence does this.

                   (Complete sentence)
                   If he had been more careful, the accident would have been avoided.

A dependent clause begins with a word like one of the following:

| after    | because | since  | until | while |
|----------|---------|--------|-------|-------|
| although | before  | that   | what  | who   |
| as       | if      | unless | which |       |

Standing on its own, a dependent clause leaves us with an unanswered question. You can see this in the next example.

**Example 2:**     (Sentence fragment)
                   Until they put a traffic light at the corner.

This clause leaves us with a question: *What will happen* until they put a traffic light at the corner?

                   (Complete sentence)
                   Until they put a traffic light at the corner, there will be more accidents.

Here is another example of a sentence fragment that is a dependent clause:

**Example 3:**     (Sentence fragment)
Who promises to put a traffic light there.

Note that in this clause, *who* is the subject of the verb *promises*. Note, also, that this clause is a statement, not a question. Standing by itself, a statement beginning with *who* does not give us enough information. To complete the sentence, we need to know more about the person that *who* refers to, as in the sentence below.

(Complete sentence)
I will vote for any politician who promises to put a traffic light there.

**Assignment:** Stories 4 and 5 contain complete sentences and sentence fragments. There is a box after each item. Write a **C** in the box if the item is a complete sentence. Write an **F** if the item is a sentence fragment. The first one is done for you.

### Story 4

A two-car accident occurred early Wednesday morning. [C] At the corner of Pearl and Mechanic streets. [ ]

A passenger in one of the cars. [ ] Alicia Alvarez sustained minor injuries. [ ] She was taken to Clinton Hospital. [ ] She was later released. [ ] After being treated for cuts and bruises. [ ]

The accident was investigated by Officer Walter Williams. [ ] Of the Clinton Police Department. [ ] He said that no charges would be filed. [ ] As a result of the accident. [ ]

In the past six months. [ ] Four accidents have occurred at the corner of Pearl and Mechanic streets. [ ] A citizens' group has been demanding a traffic light. [ ] At the busy downtown corner. [ ]

### Story 5

Firemen put out a two-alarm blaze. [ ] Yesterday at the corner of Maple and Walnut streets. [ ]

A Clinton landmark. [ ] Nora's Family Restaurant was badly damaged in the fire. [ ] Nora O'Reilly, the owner of the restaurant, estimated the damage. [ ] At $100,000. [ ]

No one was injured in the fire. [ ] Customers had already fled the restaurant. [ ] By the time the firemen arrived. [ ]

Fire departments in neighboring towns were placed on alert. [ ] Their help was not needed, however. [ ] As it turned out. [ ]

# Run-on Sentences

Two complete sentences can be joined into one sentence. The right way to join sentences is with a compound sentence. The wrong way is with a run-on sentence.

**Compound sentences are correct.** A sentence can have two or more complete thoughts. A sentence made up of two or more complete thoughts is called a compound sentence.

The complete thoughts must be connected to one another in one of two ways. One way is to use a joining word. The most common joining words are *and, but*, and *or*. The other way is to use a special punctuation mark, the semicolon (;).

> (Two complete sentences)
> Brian is a man. Mila is a woman.
>
> (Compound sentence, using a joining word)
> Brian is a man, and Mila is a woman.
>
> (Compound sentence, using a semicolon)
> Brian is a man; Mila is a woman

A compound sentence is one complete sentence. It is perfectly acceptable in writing.

**Run-on sentences are incorrect.** A sentence containing two or more complete thoughts that are not connected with a joining word or a semicolon is called a run-on sentence. A run-on sentence is not simply a long sentence; it is incorrect. Using just a comma instead of a joining word or a semicolon is a very common mistake. Run-on sentences are to be avoided in writing.

> (Run-on sentence)
> Brian is a man Mila is a woman.
>
> (Run-on sentence)
> Brian is a man, Mila is a woman.

**Assignment:** Stories 6 and 7 contain complete sentences and run-on sentences. There is a box after each item. Write a **C** in the box if the item is a complete sentence. Write an **R** if the item is a run-on sentence. The first one is done for you.

### Story 6

Alexander and Caroline Lewinski of 64 Maple Street in Clinton have announced the forthcoming marriage of their daughter Mary, she will be marrying Joseph Constantino of Springfield. ☒ R

Mary Lewinski is a graduate of Clinton High School and received an associate's degree from Howe Junior College in Milford. ☐ She is employed at the Eastern Molding Company she works as a secretary. ☐

Joseph Constantino was born in Bari, Italy; he is the son of Mrs. Sofia Constantino and the late Marco Constantino. ☐ The Constantino family came to Springfield when Joseph was five years old. ☐

Joseph graduated from Washington Street High School in Springfield. ☐ He is employed at Harold's Hardware Mart, he attends Springfield State College at night. ☐

An April wedding is planned it will be held at the Church of the Sacred Heart in Clinton. ☐

### Story 7

Twin girls were born to Mrs. Alice Martin of 47 North Street in Clinton yesterday at Clinton Hospital. ☐

One girl is being named Suzanne; the other is Pauline. ☐ Suzanne weighed 5 pounds 3 ounces at birth, Pauline, who was born 10 minutes later, weighed 4 pounds 14 ounces. ☐

The babies were delivered by Dr. Melanie Sampson of the Clinton Hospital staff. ☐ Dr. Sampson reported no complications in the twin birth, Mrs. Martin will probably be released from the hospital the day after tomorrow. ☐

The babies will remain in the hospital at least a week for observation, according to Dr. Sampson. ☐ She said that this is routine practice it does not indicate any problems. ☐

Mrs. Martin is currently on leave from her job as a teacher at Clinton High School, her husband, Charles Martin, works as an engineer with State Electric. ☐

Part A of Story 8 contains complete sentences, sentence fragments, and run-on sentences. There is a box after each item. Write a **C** in the box if the item is a complete sentence. Write an **F** if the item is a sentence fragment. Write an **R** if the item is a run-on sentence. The first one is done for you.

## Story 8: Part A

Punxsutawney Phil, the world's most famous groundhog. ☐**F** Phil saw his shadow at about seven o'clock Tuesday morning. ☐ Winter-weary Americans will be disappointed this means six more weeks of cold weather. ☐

Early reports from Punxsutawney, the western Pennsylvania town where Phil makes his home. ☐ These reports indicated that clouds blanketed the area. ☐ By seven o'clock, however, the clouds had begun to lift, the sun peeped through. ☐

A small crowd had gathered at Phil's burrow to watch the groundhog come out. ☐ The observers were unanimous, they all agreed that Phil saw his shadow. ☐

In Part B of Story 8, there are no periods to show where one sentence ends and the next one begins. Put a period at the end of each complete sentence. Also, each new sentence should begin with a capital letter. A proofreader indicates that a lowercase (small) letter should be capitalized by making three lines under it (n̲ebraska). Use the proofreader's mark to insert a capital letter at the beginning of each new sentence.

## Story 8: Part B

Punxsutawney Phil is not the only groundhog who is believed to be able to predict the weather observers in Massachusetts reported that Cochituate Chuck saw his shadow at about a quarter past six

In Wisconsin, Wausau Willie had not yet emerged from his burrow at press time reports from Wausau indicated that he would be coming out to sunny skies

According to legend, if the groundhog sees his shadow on February 2, six more weeks of winter will follow if he does not, spring will come early this legend has been traced to 19th-century German settlers in Pennsylvania in recent years Groundhog Day has been heavily promoted by chambers of commerce in several states

Part C of Story 8 contains complete sentences, sentence fragments, and run-on sentences. Correct the sentence fragments by joining them to complete sentences or by adding words to make them complete thoughts. Correct the run-on sentences by adding joining words or semicolons or by dividing them into two or more sentences.

In making these corrections, you will have to change the words and punctuation of the story. This is called "editing" the story. The marks to use in editing are shown in Instructions for Editing at the beginning of this book. You may not have to use all of the marks in editing this story.

## Story 8: Part C

The National Weather Service yesterday issued its long-range weather forecast. For February and early March.

The forecast indicates that the Northeast will have slightly milder than normal temperatures, in the Midwest, temperatures will be colder than normal. Also cold in the Pacific Northwest.

The National Weather Service and the groundhog agree. Six more weeks of winter.

HURON VALLEY SCHOOLS
ADULT EDUCATION
5061 Duck Lake Road
Highland, MI 48356

# 2. Capital Letters

Capital letters focus the reader's attention on the beginning of a sentence and on important words. When you begin a word with a capital letter, it is called capitalizing the word. Rules about capitalizing words may vary on some fine points, but there are some rules everyone agrees on. This chapter covers most of the generally accepted uses of capital letters.

## Beginning of a Sentence

**1** Capitalize the first word of a sentence.

> The phone kept ringing. Nobody answered it. After 10 rings, the caller hung up.

**2** Capitalize the first word of a quoted sentence.

> She asked him, "Why didn't you answer the phone?"
> He opened the invitation and read, "Please come to a surprise party."

**Note:** When a quotation is interrupted, the first word after the interruption is not capitalized.

> "If you come," she said, "the party will be a success."

In the example above, the word *the* is not capitalized after the interruption *she said.*

## Names of Persons

**3** Capitalize the word *I.*

> Whatever I want to do, I can do.

**4** Capitalize the name of a particular person or animal.

> Let's invite Betty and Bill to the party.
> He has a ball that was hit by Reggie Jackson.
> Many people think that Secretariat was the greatest racehorse of all time.
> Her new dog, Laddie, is a collie.

**Note:** Initials often make up part of a person's name. Initials are always capitalized.

> The truce ending the war was signed by Robert E. Lee and U.S. Grant.
> Gertrude Stein wrote about her friend Alice B. Toklas.

**5** Capitalize a title used with a person's name. Examples are *Mr., Ms., Mrs., Miss, Dr., Professor, Mayor, Senator, Colonel.*

> The two best-liked teachers in the school are Mr. Patterson and Mrs. Shaw.
> She went to Dr. Wells for her low-back pain.
> The papers were signed by Mayor Edward Johnson.

## Names of Organizations

**6** Capitalize the full name of a particular company, institution, organization, or agency.

> Since last year, the factory has been owned by General Dynamics.
> She is taking night courses at Howe Junior College.
> The memorial service is being sponsored by the Veterans of Foreign Wars.
> His tax return was audited by the Internal Revenue Service.

**Note:** When the full name is not used, the term is not capitalized. Examples are *the college, the council, the state legislature.*

> She is taking night courses at the college.
> Although she was only elected to the Clinton Town Council three months ago, she is already one of the council's most powerful members.

## Names of Places

**7** Capitalize the name of a particular place. Specifically:

**7-a** Capitalize the name of a street.

> We live on Oak Street.
> You'll get there faster if you take Courtland Road.

**7-b** Capitalize the name of a city, town, or village.

> She went to school in Boston.
> New industry is coming into Clinton.
> I never knew that cluster of houses was called East Milford.

**7-c** Capitalize the name of a county, state, province, or region.

> He's running for sheriff of Franklin County.
> It gets colder in South Dakota than it does in Missouri.
> We crossed the border and entered the province of Ontario.
> She was raised in the South and feels like a stranger in New England.

**Note:** The words *north, south, east,* and *west* are capitalized only when they refer to regions of the country. Otherwise they are written with lowercase (small) letters. Thus:

> Go six miles east on Route 44, and then go north on Route 87.

**7-d** Capitalize the name of a country.

> I have always wanted to go to France.
> He was wounded in Vietnam.
> My father was born in the United States, but his mother came from Ireland.

**7-e**    Capitalize the name of an ocean, river, lake, or other body of water.

Most of our salmon is caught in the Pacific Ocean.
The Hudson River has been polluted for many years.
The eastern part of Lake Huron is called Georgian Bay.

**7-f**    Capitalize the name of a mountain, valley, island, or park.

Even in the summertime, Mount Whitney is snow-capped.
White people settled in the Ohio Valley about 200 years ago.
She lives on Long Island and works in New York City.
We visited Yellowstone Park and didn't see any bears.

**7-g**    Capitalize a word that comes from the name of a place. Examples are *American, Californian, Chinese.*

They just bought a new Japanese car.
I think Irish setters are beautiful dogs.
Unlike many people who live in Miami, he is a native Floridian.

**Assignment:** In Part A of Story 1, words are capitalized according to rules 1 through 7-g. Above each capitalized word, there is a line. On this line, write the number (or number and letter) that tells the reason for capitalizing the word. (For example, write 3 above the word *I*.)

There may be more than one reason why a word has been capitalized. If so, write more than one number on the line. (Thus, if the name of a country comes at the beginning of a sentence, write: 1, 7-d.) The first word is done for you.

### Story 1: Part A

A dispute over a barking dog on East Street was settled last night when

Clinton Town Council ordered the animal kept inside between the hours of 9

p.m. and 8 a.m.

Neighbors said that the dog, a German shepherd named Big Boy

belonging to Karl Bower of 52 East Street, had been howling in the middle of

the night and preventing them from sleeping.

Bower, however, claimed that his dog was well-behaved and quiet. "He

didn't make any more noise than you'd expect from a dog," he told the council

meeting. "If he'd been acting bad, I would have made sure he stopped."

In Part B of Story 1, insert capital letters where needed according to rules 1 through 7-g. Use the proofreader's mark ( ＝ ) to change lowercase (small) letters to capital letters.

### Story 1: Part B

members of clinton town council and mayor edward johnson were more impressed with what they heard from linda barrett of 54 east street. "if you want to hear an unholy noise," she said, "then come over to east street some night around two o'clock.

"last week, that german shepherd didn't just wake me and my husband. he woke our baby, too. when i wasn't being kept up because of the dog, i was up because of the baby."

other neighbors had similar stories. h.j. passfield of 24 maple street said, "when big boy gets angry, the whole east side of clinton can hear him. he's a big dog. i've been way over across the black river and have heard that dog barking."

In Part C of Story 1, there are errors in the use of capital letters. The proofreader's mark indicating that a capital letter should be lowercase is a slanted line drawn through the letter (*B̸ecause*). Using both proofreader's marks ( ＝ and ／ ), edit Part C of Story 1 to correct all errors in capitalization.

### Story 1: Part C

This was not the first time a barking Dog had caused friction between bower and his neighbors. in earlier incidents, a newfoundland and a Boxer owned by the same East street resident had to be kept inside by order of clinton Town Council.

"He's had other dogs," passfield told the Council meeting, "But i think this one is the worst yet."

Members of Clinton town council agreed. They passed a motion proposed by councilor Barbara Lewis that the dog be kept inside. lewis told Bower that, if the dog was heard outside at Night again, Bower would have to pay a fine.

# Religious Terms

**8**   Capitalize certain religious terms. Specifically:

**8-a**   Capitalize the name of a religion and its followers.

He is a true Christian gentleman.
Most people in this town are Catholics.
His fiancee is a Jew, and he is converting to Judaism to marry her.
In recent years, Islam has been a more militant religion than Christianity.

**8-b**   Capitalize the name of an important religious book.

He advised the congregation to study the Bible.
The first book of the Old Testament is Genesis.
Many of the laws of Judaism are contained in the Talmud.

**8-c**   Capitalize the word *God* or any other word used to refer to the one God in any religion.

I don't understand it, but it must have been God's will.
The Lord feeds the hungry and sets the prisoner free.
Muslims pray to Allah five times a day.

**Note:** The word *god* is not capitalized when it is used in reference to a religion with many gods. Thus:

The ancient Roman god of war was Mars.

The Romans had many gods, so *god* is not capitalized. The name of a specific god, Mars, is capitalized, however.

# Time Expressions

**9**   Capitalize the names of the days of the week and the months of the year.

The fitness class meets every Monday, Wednesday, and Friday.
We usually have our coldest weather in January and February.

**Note:** The names of the seasons are not capitalized.

Football is now played in the summer, fall, and winter.

**10**   Capitalize the name of a holiday.

Two years ago, we had snow for Easter.
School begins the day after Labor Day.

**11**   Capitalize the name of an important historical event.

The French Revolution began in 1789.
A monument to soldiers killed in the Second World War stands in the town square.

**Assignment:** In Part A of Story 2, words are capitalized according to rules 1 through 11. Above each capitalized word, there is a line. On this line, write the number (or number and letter) that tells the reason for capitalizing the word. There may be more than one correct reason why a word has been capitalized. If so, write more than one number on the line.

### Story 2: Part A

All of Clinton was green on Sunday as hundreds of people turned out for the town's first-ever St. Patrick's Day parade.

Parade organizers, who had been working since last November to get the event ready, were thrilled with the response from Clinton citizens. "And most of them aren't Irish," said Grand Marshal John Kelly. "Many of them aren't even Catholic. But that doesn't matter. St. Patrick's Day is an American holiday."

The presence of Polish, Italian, and Jewish Americans among the marchers and even on the organizing committee gave support to Kelly's statement. The parade's publicity chairman, Peter Pellegrini, said, "This has to be the biggest celebration in Clinton since the Bicentennial."

In Part B of Story 2, insert capital letters where needed according to rules 1 through 11. Use the proofreader's mark ( $\underline{\underline{\phantom{m}}}$ ) to insert capital letters.

### Story 2: Part B

in his speech to the crowd on main street, kelly noted that clinton's irish community was once much larger than it is today. in the years after the civil war, irish laborers came to this area to build railroads. most of them, however, later went on to chicago, new york, or boston.

weather that seemed more like june than march brought people out and encouraged the festive spirit of the day. there was little rowdiness, with clinton police making only one arrest.

nationally, st. patrick's day was celebrated with big parades in most major cities. new york, as usual, had the largest parade.

In Part C of Story 2, there are errors in the use of capital letters. Using the proofreader's marks ( ＿ and ／ ), edit Part C of Story 2 to correct all errors in capitalization.

## Story 2: Part C

In massachusetts, State workers had monday off. That state celebrates march 17 as evacuation day, marking the Evacuation of boston by british Troops during the Revolutionary war. Many residents of Boston and worcester, with their large irish Populations, took advantage of the Holiday to attend St. Patrick's day Parades and other events.

"St. patrick's day is an American Tradition," said kelly, "And we're glad to see that clinton has joined in with it at last."

Kelly, Pellegrini, and two Assistant Organizers, stan Kiniski and Michael gallagher, all said they looked forward to an even larger Parade in Clinton next year.

## Words in Titles

**12**  Capitalize the first word, last word, and key words in a title, such as the title of a book, poem, song, play, movie, or magazine.

> I cried when I read *The Thorn Birds*.
> We had to memorize parts of *The Song of Hiawatha*.
> He has seen *Gone with the Wind* at least eight times.
> The annual baseball issue of *Sports Illustrated* is on the stands this week.

**Assignment:** In Part A of Story 3, words are capitalized according to rules 1 through 12. Above each capitalized word, there is a line. On this line, write the number (or number and letter) that tells the reason for capitalizing the word. There may be more than one correct reason why a word has been capitalized. If so, write more than one number on the line.

### Story 3: Part A

<u>   </u>
The old ways of raising a child are not always the best, according to

<u>     </u> <u>  </u>
Clinton Hospital pediatrician Dr. James V. Lyon.

<u> </u> <u>  </u>                                          <u>      </u>
Dr. Lyon was speaking to the monthly meeting of the Clinton Parents'

<u> </u>                                                              <u> </u>
Group, a club for new parents and people who are about to become parents. He

answered a wide range of questions about child care.

<u> </u>
Our parents and grandparents believed some things that modern medicine

                                                 <u> </u> <u>  </u>                      <u>  </u>
is finding out are not so, according to Dr. Lyon. As an example, he pointed out

                                                                                      <u>  </u>
that cows' milk used to be considered a good food for young babies. He said,

<u>  </u>                                                        <u>  </u>
"Many babies are allergic to cows' milk. Doctors today suggest that parents not

give their babies cows' milk until they are a year old."

<u> </u> <u>  </u>                              <u> </u> <u>     </u>      <u> </u>     <u> </u>   <u> </u>
Dr. Lyon said, however, that Dr. Benjamin Spock's *Baby and Child Care*,

written more than 40 years ago, was "still the best" book for parents to use.

---

In Part B of Story 3, insert capital letters where needed according to rules 1 through 12. Use the proofreader's mark ( ＝ ) to insert capital letters.

### Story 3: Part B

"parents who have dr. spock's book handy will save a lot of needless phone calls to the doctor," dr. lyon said. among newer books, he thinks dr. t. berry brazelton's *infants and mothers* is one of the most helpful.

another change dr. lyon noted was the growing role of fathers in taking care of their children. "ten years ago, there were very few fathers in the clinton parents' group," he said. "it should have been called the clinton mothers' group. now that has changed. it really is a parents' group."

dr. lyon also discussed progress in saving babies who used to die soon after birth. he focused on new methods developed at large hospitals such as lutheran general hospital in chicago and new york hospital.

In Part C of Story 3, there are errors in the use of capital letters. Using the proofreader's marks ( ⸗ and ╱ ), edit Part C of Story 3 to correct all errors in capitalization.

### Story 3: Part C

"Sometimes i think god must be at work in intensive care nurseries," dr. Lyon said. "what Doctors are doing there is a Miracle as great as any in the bible. Babies born three Months early and weighing less than two pounds are not only being kept alive but are growing to be normal, healthy children."

In response to a question about children's books, Dr. lyon said that very young children like Margaret wise Brown's *goodnight Moon*. For older children, he recommended A.a. Milne's Winnie-the-Pooh stories. "For the mechanically minded," he said, "A good choice is *What do people do all day?* by Richard Scarry."

After the Meeting, members of the clinton parents' group went on a tour of the maternity and children's wards in Clinton hospital.

# 3. End Punctuation

Marks that indicate the end of a sentence are called end punctuation. They also tell whether you are making a statement or asking a question. In this way, they take the place of the rise and fall of your voice when you are speaking. There are three kinds of end punctuation:

    A.  the period (.)
    B.  the question mark (?)
    C.  the exclamation point (!)

## The Period

**At the end of a sentence.** The period (.) is used at the end of a sentence that makes a statement or gives a command.

    (Statement)    It is snowing today.
    (Command)    Go outside and shovel.

In newswriting, almost all sentences are statements of fact and end with a period.

    An explosion yesterday damaged a house on Oak Street.
    The state will take over six houses so that it can build a new interchange for the state turnpike.
    Steve Garland of Mill Street spotted a moose in his back yard yesterday.

**After abbreviations.** The period or dot is sometimes used within a sentence as well. Periods are used in abbreviations. (An abbreviation is a letter or letters used as a short form of a longer word.) A period is used after each letter or group of letters that stands for a word.

Examples are: *Dr.* for *Doctor, St.* for *Street, U.S.* for *United States, tsp.* for *teaspoon.*

    Clinton Hospital has appointed Dr. Teresa Guiterrez to head its new endocrine unit. Born in Argentina, she has practiced in U.S. hospitals for 12 years.

**In numbers.** Use a dot in numbers to indicate a decimal.

    Governor Ryan has announced a new $1.2-million job-training program.
    The child's temperature was 102.4 degrees.

# The Question Mark

**At the end of questions.** The question mark (?) is used at the end of a sentence that requests an answer.

> How does it work?
> When is Easter this year?
> Is Pierre the capital of South Dakota?

**Word order in questions.** In statements, the subject usually comes before the verb. In questions, the order is often reversed. The verb comes before the subject. In the following examples, *it* is the subject and *is* is the verb.

> (Statement)    It is too cold for football today.
> (Question)    Is it too cold for football today?

Many verbs are made up of two or more words: *will play, has driven, were giving.* In such cases, only part of the verb comes before the subject in a question. In the following examples, *snow* is the subject and *will end* is the verb.

> (Statement)    The snow will end tonight.
> (Question)    When will the snow end?

**Questions in statement word order.** In some questions, the subject does come before the verb, just as in a statement. A question like this can have exactly the same words in exactly the same order as a statement. In speech, you indicate that you are asking a question by raising the pitch of your voice at the end. In writing, you put a question mark at the end.

> (Statement)
> It's time to go already. Let's get our coats.
>
> (Question)
> It's time to go already? It seems as if we just got here.

**Quoted questions.** In news stories, writers very rarely use questions. The question mark is used mostly in direct quotations, when the writer is reporting someone else's words. The person's words are in quotation marks. Note that the question mark comes before the closing quotation mark.

> The lawyer asked the witness, "Where were you on the night of March 27?"

# The Exclamation Point

**At the end of a sentence.** The exclamation point (!) is used at the end of a sentence that shows strong emotion or surprise.

> Catch the thief!
> I can't believe it!

**After sentence fragments.** An exclamation point usually comes at the end of a complete sentence. It may also follow a single word or sentence fragment. In such cases, a complete sentence usually comes just before or after the exclamation to explain its meaning.

> You tried to trick me. You old cheat!
> Brian! Come here this instant!

**In quotations.** The exclamation point is also used rarely in newswriting except in direct quotations. In quotations, it shows that the speaker has said something loudly or forcefully. Like the question mark, the exclamation point comes before the closing quotation mark.

> The angry crowd shouted: "Kill the umpire!"

**Assignment:** In Part A of Story 1, the end punctuation has been left out. Instead, there is a box at the end of each sentence. Put the correct end punctuation mark (period, question mark, or exclamation point) in each box. The first one is done for you.

### Story 1: Part A

A Clinton policeman was hospitalized yesterday after he was dragged along North Main Street by a fleeing car [.]

Officer James Tetley stopped the car when it went through a red light at the corner of Main and Mill streets [ ] He asked the driver, "Where are you going [ ]" Instead of answering, the driver shouted, "Leave me alone [ ]"

Tetley then reached in through the car's open window to arrest the driver [ ] The driver rolled up the window on Tetley's arm and stepped on the gas, dragging the policeman down the street [ ]

In Part B of Story 1, end punctuation is used incorrectly in some sentences. If an end punctuation mark is incorrect, delete it by using the proofreader's mark ( ✐ ), and insert the correct end punctuation mark. (The marks to use in editing are shown in Instructions for Editing at the beginning of this book.) The first one is done for you.

### Story 1: Part B

Another officer, Ian Holt, finally stopped the car and arrested the driver?.

Patrick Morris, 24, of Courtland has been charged with failure to stop at a red light, resisting arrest, and assaulting a police officer.

Tetley was taken to Clinton Hospital, where he is being treated for cuts and bruises on both legs. He is expected to be released today?

The injured policeman was shaken from his experience! "I've never seen anything like it," he said. "Boy, it was scary? How could anybody do such a wild thing."

In Story 2, end punctuation is used incorrectly in some sentences. If an end punctuation mark is incorrect, delete it by using the proofreader's mark ( ℘ ), and insert the correct end punctuation mark. (The marks to use in editing are shown in the Instructions for Editing at the beginning of this book.)

## Story 2

Judging by the reaction to yesterday's first Clinton showing of *TigerMan and the Invaders from Planet X*, the latest movie in the TigerMan series is going to be a box office hit!

The Spectrum Theater was filled with young viewers, mostly in the 10-to-13 age range. Several times, the action on the screen was greeted with shouts of "Wow."

This reviewer, however, wasn't as enthusiastic about the movie as the young audience was?

Is this really the kind of entertainment we want our children to be watching? How are they affected by the kind of violence they see in the TigerMan movies and others like them.

I know some people say seeing violence on the screen doesn't matter. But I read about some of the things that happen out on the street, even right here in Clinton, and I wonder?

*TigerMan and the Invaders from Planet X* is not only needlessly violent. Like the other TigerMan movies, it is also poorly acted, crudely directed, and sloppily edited!

As I left the theater, I asked myself the disturbing question, "This is the best Hollywood can do."

# Part 2
# Internal Punctuation

When you speak, the pitch of your voice and the pauses between words help to make your meaning clear to the listener. Internal punctuation helps make the meaning of a written sentence clear to the reader. There are nine internal punctuation marks:

| | | |
|---|---|---|
| , | A. | The comma |
| ; | B. | The semicolon |
| : | C. | The colon |
| — | D. | The dash |
| ( ) | E. | Parentheses |
| - | F. | The hyphen |
| , | G. | The apostrophe |
| " " | H. | Quotation marks |
| ' ' | I. | Single quotation marks |

In the next five chapters, we will look at these internal punctuation marks one by one and see how to use them.

# 4. The Comma

The comma (,) is the most common internal punctuation mark. Commas are used to separate groups of words from other groups of words in a sentence. Their purpose is to keep the reader from getting confused.

## Commas That Separate Items

### Items in a series

A-1    Use a comma to separate items in a series. (A series is a list of more than two items.)

> Cheese omelets, oatmeal muffins, coffee cake, and sausage will be served at the breakfast.

**Note:** Don't use a comma after the last item in a series.

> (Wrong)    Property taxes, street repairs, and the new bridge, will be on the agenda at tonight's meeting.

> (Right)    Property taxes, street repairs, and the new bridge will be on the agenda at tonight's meeting.

### Two adjectives

A-2    Use a comma to separate two or more adjectives that describe the same thing when the two adjectives could be connected by the word *and*.

> The tired, hungry Cub Scouts returned home after their hike.

Note that *tired, hungry Cub Scouts* could be replaced by *tired and hungry Cub Scouts*.

**Note:** When the two adjectives cannot be connected by the word *and*, no comma is used.

> He wears a grey flannel suit to work.

Here, you could not substitute *grey and flannel suit.*

## Commas That Separate Parts of Sentences

### Tag questions

A-3    A tag question begins with a statement and then adds a tag at the end that turns it into a question. Use a comma between the two parts.

> It has been a long winter, hasn't it?

### Direct quotations

A-4    Use commas to set off words like *he said* from a direct quotation. (A direct quotation gives the exact words of the person who said it.)

> "I wonder," he said, "if spring will ever come."

## Compound sentences

**A-5**  Use a comma between the two parts of a compound sentence that are joined by the word *and, but, or, nor, for,* or *yet.*

(A compound sentence is made up of two or more complete thoughts. Each part could stand alone as a sentence. When they are joined in a compound sentence, the parts are called independent clauses.)

> The school board will meet tonight, and the town council will meet tomorrow night.
>
> The Tigers scored four touchdowns and three field goals, yet they lost the game 38-36.

**Note 1:** Don't use a comma between two parts of a compound **subject** or compound **verb.**

> (Wrong)  The president of Glencoe Electronics Company, and the junior senator from Iowa will be among the speakers.
>
> (Right)  The president of Glencoe Electronics Company and the junior senator from Iowa will be among the speakers.
>
> (Wrong)  I saw a unicorn right in my own backyard, and actually touched its horn.
>
> (Right)  I saw a unicorn right in my own backyard and actually touched its horn.

**Note 2:** Don't use a comma after *and, but, or, nor, for,* or *yet.*

> (Wrong)  All town offices will be closed Monday, but, banks will be open from 9 a.m. to noon.
>
> (Right)  All town offices will be closed Monday, but banks will be open from 9 a.m. to noon.

## Introductory phrases and dependent clauses

**A-6**  A comma is used to set off a prepositional phrase at the beginning of a sentence. A prepositional phrase begins with a word like *in, on, after, for,* or *without.*

> After the meeting, everyone went home.
> On Columbus Day, the stores will be open.

A comma may be used to set off an introductory phrase like *Next week, Last winter,* or *Later that day.*

> Next week, we are invited to a party.

Always use a comma after a dependent clause at the beginning of a sentence. Dependent clauses begin with a word like *after, although, as, because, before, if, since, unless, until,* or *while.*

> Although Councilor Lewis is opposed to higher property taxes, she is willing to compromise on the issue.
>
> Unless negotiators can work out an agreement this evening, there will be a strike tomorrow morning.
>
> Until repairs to Highway 21 are completed, drivers will have to use Old Courtland Road instead.

# Commas That Set Off Interruptions

Commas are used to set off an expression that interrupts the sentence. Such an expression provides extra information, but it can be left out without destroying the meaning of the sentence.

If the interruption comes in the middle of the sentence, a comma is used before it and after it.

### Clauses with *who* and *which*

**A-7**    Use commas to set off a clause beginning with *who* or *which* if it can be left out without destroying the meaning of the sentence.

> The new mayor, who will be elected next Tuesday, will appoint the chief of police.

If the expression between commas is left out, the sentence still makes sense.

> The new mayor will appoint the chief of police.

Here is another example:

> He got a job with Contemporary Data Processing, which is the fastest-growing company in town.

The sentence still makes sense without the *which* clause.

> He got a job with Contemporary Data Processing.

In the following sentence, however, no commas are used because the information in the *who* clause is necessary to the sentence.

> A person who cannot do math should not be working in a bank.

Without the dependent clause, the sentence does not make sense:

> A person should not be working in a bank.

**Note:** Commas are never used to set off a dependent clause that begins with *that* or *what*.

> The table that used to be in the living room is now in the garage.
> She said what was on her mind quietly but firmly.

### Appositives

**A-8**    Use commas to set off an appositive. An appositive is a word or group of words that renames a person, place, or thing.

> The mayor of Clinton, Edward Johnson, spoke at the ceremony.

In this sentence, *Edward Johnson* is another way of identifying *the mayor of Clinton*.

> She came from Woodstock, the smallest town in the county.

In the last sentence, *the smallest town in the county* is another way of identifying *Woodstock*.

### Other interruptions

**A-9**    Use commas to set off other interruptions if the sentence would still make sense without them. Some examples are *yes, no, oh, well, however, of course,* and *in fact.*

> Oh, we will be at the party at eight o'clock.
>
> We will have to leave early, however, because we promised the baby-sitter we would be home by eleven.
>
> Parents of small children, in fact, are seldom able to stay out late.
>
> Indeed, they are seldom able to go out at all.

Use commas to set off the name of a person spoken to or other words that refer to that person.

> Paul, would you help me with the dishes?
>
> I just remembered, my dear, that this is our anniversary.

Use commas to set off a phrase beginning with *not* that contrasts with some other word or words in the sentence.

> Honey, not vinegar, is what catches flies.
>
> Wear your long underwear and a heavy jacket, not your summer T-shirts and shorts, if you plan to go fishing in October.

**Assignment:** In Part A of Story 1, note the use of each comma. On the line above each comma, write the letter and number from rules A-1 through A-9. The first one is done for you.

### Story 1: Part A

The Clinton baseball Tigers mounted a ninth-inning rally yesterday, *(A-5)* but it wasn't enough to win the annual game against the Raiders from West Auburn High School.

The Raiders, who are undefeated so far this season, scored five runs in the third inning on their way to an 11-6 victory. Ken Clark, Tim Gray, and Willie Jamieson all hit home runs for West Auburn.

In the middle of the ninth inning, the Raiders led 11-2. A triple by Jim Turner, a long, looping single by John MacDonald, and a double by Carl Abbott in the Clinton half of the ninth brought the crowd to its feet.

At this point, the West Auburn coach, Doc Harris, took out his starting pitcher, Dave Ilsley, and brought in Tom Kroll, the star Raider reliever.

In Part B of Story 1, insert commas where needed according to rules A-1 through A-9. The first one is done for you.

## Story 1: Part B

Kroll struck out Ron Bowell,but Jack Tupper continued the rally with a double that scored MacDonald and Abbott. At this point the Tiger coach Steve Borden sent a pinch-hitter Don Bracken to the plate.

Bracken hit a long high fly ball that got away from Stan Fielding the Raider right fielder. Bracken however tried to take three bases and Fleming threw him out at third. Tupper scored on the play and the score stood at 11-6.

Kroll who has saved four games for the Raiders this season then retired the next Clinton hitter Ed Dinsdale on a routine grounder and the Raiders had won the Clinton-West Auburn game for the third year in a row.

Edit Part C of Story 1 by inserting commas where needed and deleting commas that are not needed. Use the proofreader's mark ( ℓ ) to delete commas (John͗Doe). Follow rules A-1 through A-9 for the use of commas.

## Story 1: Part C

Tim Gray, who hit two singles as well as his home run was named the outstanding player, of the game. Four of the seven judges, voted for Gray. Ken Clark Dave Ilsley, and Tom Kroll, each received one vote.

"I think the judges made a fine choice" said a happy, Coach Borden.

Next Saturday Clinton faces, the Plainville High School Bluebirds, in Plainville. West Auburn goes on to meet the Greenfield Flyers and the outcome of that game, could determine the County League championship.

Chuck Lang who allowed only six hits in beating York, will be the starting pitcher, for the Tigers. Bill Basford, a left-hander will start for the Bluebirds.

# Conventional Uses of the Comma

A custom that many people agree on is called a convention. The following are called conventional uses of the comma.

### Dates

**A-10**  Use commas to separate the parts of a date. The parts are:

— the name of the day of the week (Friday)
— the month plus the date of the month (November 22)
— the year (1963)

When the date comes at the beginning or in the middle of a sentence, there must be another comma after it.

> Friday, November 22, is a day I will never forget.
> President John F. Kennedy was assassinated on November 22, 1963, in Dallas.

**Note:** Don't use a comma between the month and the date of the month.

> (Wrong)   My vacation begins on July, 19.
> (Right)   My vacation begins on July 19.

### Place names and addresses

**A-11**  Use a comma between the name of a city or town and its state or country.

> The Wright brothers flew the first airplane in Kitty Hawk, North Carolina.
> He was born in 1946 in Cracow, Poland.

When the place name comes in the middle of a sentence, there must be another comma after the name of the state or country.

> They lived in Dayton, Ohio, before they moved here.
> She is working in Calcutta, India, at the American embassy.

On a letter or envelope, an address is written on separate lines. Only one comma is needed—between the city and state.

> Mr. Henry Jones
> 325 Blakemore St.
> Minneapolis, Minnesota 55436

When a full address is part of a sentence, use a comma after the street address and after the city name.

> Jones gave his address as 325 Blakemore St., Minneapolis, Minnesota 55436.

### Greeting of friendly letter

**A-12**  Use a comma after the greeting of a friendly letter.

> Dear Rosa,
>
> I'll be glad to come to your party.

### Closing of a letter

**A-13**  Use a comma after the closing of any letter.

> Yours truly,                    Or:       Love,
>
> *William Moore*                           *Bill*
>
> William Moore

**Assignment:** In Letter 1, note the use of each comma. On the line above each comma, write the letter and number from rules A-1 through A-13.

## Letter 1

475 Water Street

Louisville, ¯ Kentucky 40211

June 4, ¯ 1990

Dear Phil, ¯

I am looking for a new job, ¯ and I am hoping that you will be able to help me find one. As you may remember, ¯ I worked on newspapers in Jackson, ¯ Michigan, ¯ and Columbus, ¯ Indiana, ¯ before I got this public relations job in Louisville. I've decided I don't really like public relations. Moreover, ¯ city life is not for me.

Do you know if there are going to be any openings at the *Clinton Daily News*? Please let me know if there are any. I would love working on a small-town newspaper again, ¯ and being in the same town as you would be an added bonus.

Best regards, ¯

*Judy*

In Letter 2, insert commas following rules A-1 through A-13.

**Letter 2**

## CLINTON DAILY NEWS

June 9 1990

Dear Judy

Actually one of our reporters is going to be leaving at the end of August. With your experience Judy you would have a good chance of getting the job. Send a letter your resume and some articles you've written to the managing editor Fred Westcott. He used to work in Bloomington Indiana which is not far from Columbus and he's probably familiar with the paper you wrote for.

I am also excited about the possibility that we might be in the same area again. If you're coming here for an interview you can stay at my place.

Cheers

*Phil*

Edit Letter 3 by inserting commas where needed and deleting commas that are not needed. Follow rules A-1 through A-13.

## Letter 3

475, Water Street
Louisville Kentucky 40211
June, 29, 1990

Dear Phil

My interview with Mr. Westcott is scheduled for Friday July, 26. I have to be in Joplin Missouri, for another interview on Wednesday July 31 but, I can spend a few days in Clinton before I go.

I'm looking forward to seeing you. It's been a whole year, that we haven't seen each other. I can't believe it's been that long can you?

Best, regards

Judy

# 5. The Semicolon and the Colon

In this chapter, we will look at two more internal punctuation marks: the semicolon and the colon.

## B: The Semicolon

A semicolon (;) marks a more important break in the sentence than a comma does. The following are specific uses of the semicolon:

### In compound sentences

**B-1**  Use a semicolon between independent clauses when the clauses are **not** joined by one of these conjunctions (linking words): *and, but, for, or, nor,* or *yet.*

> Clinton observed Memorial Day yesterday with a ceremony in the town square; the ceremony honored Clinton's war dead.

> Mayor Johnson was the first speaker; he was followed by Rev. Charles Axworthy.

**Note:** Words like *accordingly, also, besides, however, then, therefore,* and *thus* are not conjunctions (linking words). They are adverbs that modify, or describe, the verb in the clause. When one of these adverbs is used between clauses, there should be a semicolon before it.

In the following sentence, *accordingly* is an adverb that modifies the verb *was chosen.* A semicolon is needed between the two independent clauses because they are not joined by a linking word.

> Rev. Axworthy has the largest congregation in town; accordingly, he was chosen to deliver the opening prayer.

### Between independent clauses

**B-2**  Use a semicolon between independent clauses joined by the linking words *and, but, for, or, nor,* and *yet* when there are several commas within the clauses.

> Mayor Johnson praised the valor of the Clinton men who fought in the First World War, the Second World War, the Korean War, and the Vietnam War, and urged the audience to honor the memories of those who died in those conflicts; and then Rev. Axworthy thanked God that no Clinton men were fighting overseas today.

The semicolon helps the reader see which parts of this complicated sentence belong with the first clause and which parts belong with the second clause.

### Between items in a series

**B-3**  Use a semicolon between items in a series when the items themselves contain commas.

> Town Councilors Barbara Lewis, George Douglas, and Harold Coldwell; Elliott Woodsworth, Clinton's representative in the state legislature; and Rabbi Joseph Goldbloom, spiritual leader of Congregation Beth David, were also present at the ceremony.

In this complicated list, the semicolons help the reader tell how many persons were present.

# C: The Colon

A colon (:) is used to mean "note what follows." These are specific uses of the colon:

### To introduce a list

**C-1**  Use a colon to introduce a list of items if the words before the list make up a complete sentence.

> Mayor Johnson mentioned some of the battles in which Clinton men had fought: Soissons, Iwo Jima, Inchon, and Khe Sanh.

> Then he talked about some of those who had died in Vietnam: Jack Lawrence, Pete Flynn, Jerry McGrath, and Steve Davis.

If the introduction is not a complete sentence, and the items in the list are needed to make it complete, do not use a colon.

> Then he talked about Jack Lawrence, Pete Flynn, Jerry McGrath, and Steve Davis.

### To introduce a quotation

**C-2**  A colon may be used to introduce a quotation if the words before the quotation make up a complete sentence.

> Mayor Johnson concluded with a wish: "May we always be able to remember these brave men in times of peace."

### To link independent clauses

**C-3**  Use a colon before a clause that explains the preceding clause.

> The mayor made a good speech: that is, he said what I would have said.
> I thought Councilor Coldwell's speech was the best: he made me feel proud of the boys who fought in faraway places.

### After greeting in a business letter

**C-4**  Use a colon after the greeting in a business letter.

> Dear Manager:
>
> I wish to register a complaint about my telephone service.

> Dear Ms. Lewis:
>
> A traffic light is needed at the corner of Oak and Mill streets. The residents of our neighborhood would like you to bring this issue to the attention of the town council.

**Between hour and minutes**

**C-5** Use a colon between the hour and the minutes in time expressions.

> The ceremony began at 3:30 p.m. and concluded at 4:45.

**Between chapter and verse**

**C-6** Use a colon between chapter and verse in references to the Bible.

> Rev. Axworthy quoted from Isaiah 2:4, "Nation shall not lift sword against nation nor ever again be trained for war."

**Assignment:** In Part A of Story 1, there is a line above each semicolon and colon. On the line, note the use of each semicolon or colon. Write the correct letter and number from the list above (B-1 through C-6). The first one is done for you.

### Story 1: Part A

Alice Pennell has been named Clinton's Most Outstanding Citizen of the
Year; *B-1* the award honors her fund-raising work for Clinton Hospital.

Pennell has led three major fund-raising drives for the hospital: a campaign
eight years ago, which resulted in the building of the Buchanan Wing; another
campaign five years ago, which allowed the hospital to purchase modern
diagnostic equipment; and last year's campaign, which raised $100,000 for new
surgical facilities.

The announcement of the award was released yesterday by the mayor's
office; it praised Pennell for her "devotion to the hospital that she has helped
make into an outstanding institution."

The announcement quoted Hebrews 13:16, "Do not neglect to do good and
to share what you have, for such sacrifices are pleasing to God"; and it said
that Pennell has lived up to the Biblical verse "in full measure."

Part B of Story 1 is written without internal punctuation. Insert commas, semicolons, and colons where needed according to rules A-1 through C-6.

## Story 1: Part B

Pennell is a member of the board of directors of Clinton Hospital. She is also a director of the Clinton Opportunity Council.

Born Alice Campbell in Chicago she came to Clinton with her family when she was nine. She married Walter Pennell now a teacher at Clinton High School in 1956. The Pennells have three children Linda a nurse at Clinton Hospital Caroline a junior at Washington University in St. Louis and George a senior at Clinton High School.

The Most Outstanding Citizen of the Year is chosen by a panel of judges appointed by the mayor's office. This year the judges were Arthur Fulton editor of the *Daily News* Clinton's state representative Elliott Woodsworth and Ann Kirkland a local attorney.

Edit Part C of Story 1 for commas, semicolons, and colons according to rules A-1 through C-6. Insert commas, semicolons, and colons where needed. Delete or change punctuation marks that are wrong. Use the proofreader's mark ( ⌿ ) to delete punctuation marks (Jane͜ Doe).

## Story 1: Part C

In addition to Pennell the panel chose three other Outstanding Citizens; Albert McLean chairman of the Beautify Clinton Committee, Ray Stevens scoutmaster at All Saints Church, and Ella Timbrell coach of the county champion girls' basketball team.

Attached to the announcement from the mayor's office was a letter from Governor Ryan. The letter read:

Dear Mayor Johnson;

I am pleased to join with you in honoring Clinton's Outstanding Citizens. Men and women such as Alice Pennell; Albert McLean; Ray Stevens; and Ella Timbrell have helped make this state great; and I am proud of them.

Yours truly:

Kevin Ryan

The Outstanding Citizen awards will be presented to Pennell McLean Stevens and Timbrell today in a ceremony at the Town Hall. The ceremony will begin at 2.30 p.m.

In Letter 1, there is a line above each semicolon and colon. On this line, note the use of each semicolon or colon. Write the correct letter and number from the list above (B-1 through C-6).

**Letter 1**

140 North Street

Clinton, Anystate 12345

April 3, 2000

Dr. Melanie Sampson

Medical Arts Wing

Clinton Hospital

Clinton, Anystate 12345

Dear Dr. Sampson‾:

    I will be unable to keep my appointment with you at 3‾:30 p.m. on April ‾16‾; could you please reschedule it for another time,   preferably before 1‾1‾:30 a.m. on Friday, April 18?

Yours truly,

*Heather Notley*

Heather Notley

In Letter 2, insert commas, semicolons, and colons where needed according to rules A-1 through C-6.

**Letter 2**

Medical Arts Wing
Clinton Hospital
Clinton Anystate 12345
April 6 2000

Ms. Heather Notley
140 North Street
Clinton Anystate 12345

Dear Ms. Notley

The only time we have available on the morning of Friday April 18 is 8 45 a.m. Please let us know if that is convenient for you. If it is not we will have to delay the appointment until next month.

Yours truly

*Catherine Kelly*

Catherine Kelly, R.N.
for Dr. Melanie Sampson

Edit Letter 3 for commas, semicolons, and colons according to rules A-1 through C-6. Insert commas, semicolons, and colons where needed. Delete or change punctuation marks that are wrong.

**Letter 3**

140 North Street

Clinton Anystate 12345

April 10 2000

Ms. Catherine Kelly, R.N.

c/o Dr. Melanie Sampson

Medical Arts Wing

Clinton Hospital

Clinton Anystate 12345

Dear Ms. Kelly,

I will be able to keep the appointment at 8;45 a.m. on Friday April, 18. Thank you for accommodating me.

Yours truly;

*Heather Notley*

Heather Notley

# 6. Dashes and Parentheses

Dashes and parentheses are both used to set off something that breaks the flow of thought in a sentence.

## D: The Dash

A dash (—) indicates a significant break in the thought. If the interruption comes in the middle of a sentence, use one dash before it and another dash after it. When using a typewriter, make a dash by typing two hyphens: (--). The following are specific uses of the dash:

**D-1**   Use a dash to show an abrupt break in thought.

> The Memorial Day ceremony—but not the weather, I'm sorry to say—was beautiful.
>
> The mayor's speech moved many people in the crowd to tears—loud claps of thunder also startled them.

**D-2**   Use a dash to set off extra information that is not closely related to the main sentence.

> Councilor Barbara Lewis—at 32, the youngest member of the town council—was the last speaker of the day.
>
> Her speech—delivered as rain began to fall—was about the need to prevent future wars.

**D-3**   Use a dash to mean *namely, in other words,* or *that is.*

> Seven hundred people attended the ceremony—about a hundred fewer than last year.

## E: Parentheses

**E**   Use parentheses ( ) to enclose information that is added to a sentence but is not considered of major importance.

> The Clinton War Memorial (one of the largest in the state) was built as a monument to Clinton men who died in the First World War.
>
> A new plaque (made out of stone quarried in Clinton) was recently added to honor the memory of local boys who died in Vietnam.

# Commas, Dashes, or Parentheses?

Often, you have a choice of using commas, dashes, or parentheses to set off material that interrupts the main sentence. As a general rule, commas are used to set off material that is closely related to the rest of the sentence. Material set off between dashes is less closely related to the rest of the sentence, and material in parentheses much less so.

Also, you should use dashes or parentheses if the interruption contains commas or if it forms a complete sentence.

> The Elm Street playground, with its baseball diamond and swings, is a favorite gathering place for Clinton's children.
>
> The Elm Street playground—until 10 years ago, it was a vacant lot—is a favorite gathering place for Clinton's children.
>
> The Elm Street playground (across the street from where my grandparents lived when they first came to Clinton) is a favorite gathering place for Clinton's children.

**Assignment:** In Part A of Story 1, note the use of each semicolon, colon, dash, or set of parentheses. On the line above each punctuation mark, write the letter and number of the rule that applies, using rules B-1 through E.

## Story 1: Part A

Author Jean McNair will speak Thursday night at the regular meeting of the Clinton Historical Society. Her topic will be "The Depression in Clinton—a Time of Hardship."

The meeting will begin at 8:30 p.m. (one hour later than the society's usual meeting time). McNair will be introduced by Historical Society president—and local businessman—Michael Wells.

McNair—a native of Clinton, but a resident of New York City for 30 years—has had eight books published. Her latest book is *No One Called Us Poor*; it is her second collection of sketches of Clinton during her childhood.

Part B of Story 1 is written without internal punctuation. Insert commas, semicolons, colons, dashes, and parentheses where needed according to rules A-1 through E.

## Story 1: Part B

Besides her earlier book of childhood memories *Far from the Towers* McNair's books include *Season of Sorrows* a novel set in a small midwestern town during the Second World War *Gideon and Other Heroes* a collection of short stories and *Reaching for the Top* a book about New York.

In addition McNair has written several TV screenplays and many articles for *Ladies' Home Journal* and *New York* magazine.

This will be the first time in seven years that she has been in Clinton except for a brief visit on her way to Los Angeles a year ago.

Edit Part C of Story 1 for commas, semicolons, colons, dashes, and parentheses. Follow rules A-1 through E. Insert commas, semicolons, colons, dashes, and parentheses where needed. Delete or change punctuation marks that are wrong.

## Story 1: Part C

After this week's meeting the Clinton Historical Society is planning three more programs before the summer; on April, 19; May, 24; and June, 21.

The April meeting will be entitled—"America before the White Man." The May meeting at which a new executive will be elected will discuss railroads in Clinton, a number of possibilities are being considered for the June meeting.

Thursday night's meeting will be held in the Hincks Memorial Room— formerly the Clinton Room, in the Clinton Public Library.

# 7. The Hyphen and the Apostrophe

In this chapter, we will look at two internal punctuation marks that are used often. They are the hyphen and the apostrophe.

## F: The Hyphen

The hyphen (-) has a number of uses:

### In compound numbers

**F-1**  Use a hyphen to write compound numbers from *twenty-one* to *ninety-nine*.

> Thirty-four dollars is the price before tax.
> Two hundred seventy-seven new students enrolled in the Clinton schools this year.

### In fractions used as modifiers

**F-2**  Use a hyphen between the two parts of a spelled-out fraction that is used as a modifier.

> She was elected by a two-thirds majority.
> Ninety and one-half inches is the length of the sofa.

**Note:** If the fraction is used as a noun, do not use a hyphen.

> More than one half of the class is male.
> She cut the pie into thirds, and he ate two thirds.

### With inclusive numbers

**F-3**  Use a hyphen to write inclusive numbers or dates.

> The factory prospered during World War I (1914-1918).
> In some schools, drug use is becoming common among preteen students (those 10-12 years old).

### After some prefixes

**F-4**  Use a hyphen after a prefix in certain cases:

**F-4-a**  Use a hyphen between a prefix and a capitalized word.

> It is not anti-American to criticize the government.
> The non-Catholic population of Clinton is increasing.

**F-4-b**  Use a hyphen between a prefix and a number.

> In pre-1914 Europe, most countries had kings or emperors.
> The post-1970 period saw great progress in Clinton.

### To join words

**F-5**  Use a hyphen to make a new word out of two or more existing words.

> The mayor-elect thanked his supporters.
> There are thirty-odd bars in this town.
> Karen Bond was elected president of the club, and Wilbur Smith was elected secretary-treasurer.
> You don't often see a jack-in-the-pulpit around here.
> I don't know of a more thirst-quenching drink than cranberry juice.

**Note:** There are no absolute rules about when to join words with a hyphen. Hyphens are used most commonly:

**F-5-a**  when a group of words is used regularly in a special sense (*jack-in-the-pulpit, ne'er-do-well*).

**F-5-b**  when a group of words is used as an adjective before a noun. Examples are *an up-to-date method, a well-liked teacher, a half-naked man.*

If the group of words comes *after* the noun, it is not hyphenated. Thus:

> She is a well-known singer.
> The singer is well known.

### At the end of a line

**F-6**  Use a hyphen to divide a word at the end of a line. The break must come at the end of a syllable. A syllable contains one vowel sound.

> Pam decided she was spending too much time watching television, so now she is learning data processing in her free time.

> While agriculture and mining are still important, manufacturing now employs the most people in the county.

**Assignment:** In Part A of Story 1, note the use of each hyphen. On the line, write the letter and number from the list above (F-1 through F-6). Note only the main rules (such as F-4), and do not worry about the sub-rules (such as F-4-a). The first one is done for you.

### *F-3* Story 1: Part A

In the decade 1970-1980, Clinton's population grew by 3,752 to 24,876, according to census figures released yesterday.

The largest increase was in the American-born sector of the population, which grew from 14,957 in 1970 to 17,789 in 1980. The number of foreign-born people in Clinton grew more slowly, from 6,167 in 1970 to 7,087 in 1980.

Catholics remained by far the largest religious group at 16,124. There was a large increase in the number of non-Catholics, however. Non-Catholics now represent more than one third of the town's population for the first time in seventy-five years.

Part B of Story 1 is written without internal punctuation (except commas in numbers and quotation marks). Insert commas, semicolons, colons, dashes, parentheses, and hyphens where needed according to rules A-1 through F-6.

### Story 1: Part B

As for age groups the 0 19 group the largest in 1970 is now second to the 20 39 group. This change which follows an America wide trend is due to the aging of the baby boom generation born in the years 1945 1955.

Another change noted by the census is a large increase in the 60 and over group which now makes up more than one fifth of the population.

The census also shows that the population of Clinton is better off than it used to be with an average family income of $19,384. This figure increased by $7,859 in the 1970 1980 period.

Paul Cullen vice president of the Clinton Chamber of Commerce said the population increased because of the growth of industry in town. He said that "it is a well known fact that industry makes a town grow. Clinton is proof of that."

Edit Part C of Story 1 for internal punctuation according to rules A-1 through F-6. Insert internal punctuation where needed. Delete or change punctuation marks that are wrong.

## Story 1: Part C

Cullen noted that most of Clinton's population-growth has taken place in the post 1945 period. "Thirty five years ago," he said, "Clinton was a one industry, low income, no growth town. Since then, it has really taken-off."

According to Cullen the increase in average-income is further proof that Clinton is "an up to date, progressive town."

The census confirms Cullen's-belief that industry is the source of Clinton's growth. A total of 6,191 Clintonians—almost one quarter of the population—are employed in industry. Almost-one-half of the people in the 20 39 and 40 59 age-groups have industrial jobs.

# G: The Apostrophe

The apostrophe ( ' ) is used in the following ways:

### To show possession

**G-1** Use an apostrophe to show possession in these ways:

**G-1-a** Add -'s to singular nouns.

He tripped on the child's toy.
You can get anything you want at Alice's restaurant.
I married the boss's daughter, and now I am vice-president of the company.

**G-1-b** Add an apostrophe ( ' ) to plural nouns with the -s ending.

The Robertsons' new car is a Toyota.
The directors' meeting has been postponed.
The governor said it was an issue of states' rights.

**G-1-c** Add -'s to plural nouns that do not have the -s ending.

The Children's Zoo is closed on Tuesdays.
The men's room is to your left, and the women's room is down the hall.

**Note 1:** Even if a singular name ends with *s, z,* or *x,* you still add -'s to show possession.

| | |
|---|---|
| Tom Jones's songs | Liz's diamonds |
| Joe Louis's fights | Groucho Marx's cigar |

Exceptions are the names *Jesus* and *Moses* and names ending in *es* pronounced *eez.* Just add an apostrophe to these names.

in Jesus' name      Moses' leadership      Hermes' sandals

**Note 2:** If two or more people own the same item jointly, use the ending -'s only on the last of the names you mention.

| | |
|---|---|
| Bob and Mary's house | Mr. and Mrs. Johnson's children |
| my aunt and uncle's car | Tom, Ed, and Sue's trip to Utah |

If each person owns something by himself, use the ending -'s on each name.

Bob's and Mary's shoes      my aunt's and uncle's toothbrushes

### To stand for letters omitted

**G-2** Use an apostrophe to show where letters have been omitted:

**G-2-a** in certain abbreviations.

Yes, ma'am [madam], I did take an apple from your tree.
The meeting will begin at nine o'clock [of the clock].
Tim is afraid of snakes and 'gators [alligators].

**G-2-b** in contractions. A contraction is made up of two words run together. (See the list of contractions on the next page.)

We're [We are] leaving on Thursday, but with the weather so uncertain we can't [cannot] tell when we'll [we will] arrive.

**Note:** *It's* is a contraction meaning *it is* or *it has*. The possessive form of *it* is written without an apostrophe: *its*.

It's [It is] a beautiful day today.
It's [It has] been a long time since it was so warm in April.
St. Michael's Church is a Clinton landmark because you can see its steeple from anywhere in town.

### To form plurals

**G-3** Use an apostrophe to form the plural of a letter, a symbol, or an abbreviation with periods.

There are two *s*'s in the word *lassie*.
The *Daily News* gave the Silver Moon four +'s, its highest rating for restaurants.
He has two B.A.'s, one in English and one in history.

**Note:** An apostrophe is not needed to form the plural of a numeral or of an abbreviation without periods. Simply add the ending *-s*.

In the 1950s, few homes had two TVs.

# Contractions

A contraction is made up of two words that are run together. An apostrophe stands for the letters that are omitted from one of the words.

**am**
I'm = I am

**are**
you're = you are
we're = we are
they're = they are

**is, has**
he's = he is *or* he has
she's = she is *or* she has
it's = it is *or* it has

what's = what is *or* what has
that's = that is *or* that has
who's = who is *or* who has
there's = there is *or* there has
here's = here is

**have**
I've = I have
you've = you have
we've = we have
they've = they have

could've = could have
would've = would have
should've = should have

**would, had**
I'd = I would *or* I had
you'd = you would *or* you had
he'd = he would *or* he had
she'd = she would *or* she had
it'd = it would *or* it had
we'd = we would *or* we had
they'd = they would *or* they had

**will**
I'll = I will
you'll = you will
he'll = he will
she'll = she will
it'll = it will
we'll = we will
they'll = they will
that'll = that will

**us**
let's = let us

**not**
isn't = is not
aren't = are not

wasn't = was not
weren't = were not

doesn't = does not
don't = do not
didn't = did not

won't = will not

hasn't = has not
haven't = have not
hadn't = had not

mustn't = must not

can't = cannot

couldn't = could not
wouldn't = would not
shouldn't = should not

**Assignment:** In Part A of Story 2, there are lines above some internal punctuation marks. On each line, note the use of the punctuation mark. Write the letter and number of the rule, from A-1 through G-3. Note the main rules only (such as G-1); do not worry about sub-rules (such as G-1-a).

### Story 2: Part A

Mrs. Jennie Rose of Maple Street in Clinton wept with joy yesterday as she was reunited with her brother and sister-in-law. She hadn't seen them in thirty-six years.

"It's a dream come true," Mrs. Rose said. Her brother, Marek Paszczkowski of Katowice, Poland, and his wife, Katrina, arrived in Clinton yesterday. They came to visit Mrs. Rose, who left Poland in 1948.

Marek and Jennie's parents and other members of their family were killed in Nazi-occupied Poland during World War II. "They're the only family I've got left," says Mrs. Rose. "We've missed each other terribly."

Part B of Story 2 is written without internal punctuation except for quotation marks and commas that set off direct quotations. Insert internal punctuation marks where needed according to rules A-1 through G-3.

### Story 2: Part B

The Paszczkowskis also met their brother in law Frank Rose and the Roses three children for the first time yesterday. American born of Polish parents Frank married Jennie in Clinton in 1956.

Frank and Jennies daughter Anna made the arrangements for the Paszczkowskis to come to America. "Shes a wonderful girl," said Mrs. Rose. "Without Annas help this wouldnt have happened."

Anna paid part of the Paszczkowskis plane fare helped them get the necessary papers and met them at Kennedy International Airport in New York. She spent an anxious hour at the airport while officials looked over her aunt and uncles papers before allowing them to enter the United States.

"I think the officials just had trouble with a name that had all those *z*s and *k*s," Anna said. "Uncle Marek and Aunt Katrinas papers were completely in order."

Edit Part C of Story 2 for internal punctuation according to rules A-1 through G-3. Insert internal punctuation where needed. Delete or change punctuation marks that are wrong.

## Story 2: Part C

Annas' two brothers Stan and James also helped to pay for the Paszczkowskis trip.

Tonight the Roses' will have a traditional Polish American family-dinner. Franks mother Marya Rose, will be arriving from Milwaukee this afternoon, to meet her daughter in laws' long lost relatives.

The Paszczkowski's will be spending the next two-weeks' in Clinton. After that they and the Roses' will visit New York Philadelphia, and Washington D.C.

"I hope Frank and I can go to Poland during next years vacation," said Mrs. Rose. "W'ed love to see Marek and Katrinas' home in Katowice. We want this to be the first of many visits."

# 8. Quotation Marks

In this chapter, we will look at the last two internal punctuation marks. They are quotation marks and single quotation marks. The last part of this chapter will tell how to use quotation marks along with other punctuation marks.

## H: Quotation Marks

Quotation marks (" ") are used to set off quotations and some kinds of titles. The following are specific uses of quotation marks:

### Quotations

**H-1**   Enclose the exact words of another speaker or writer in quotation marks. The exact words are called a direct quotation.

> My mother always told me, "Never talk to strangers."
> As Shakespeare wrote, "To thine own self be true."

**Note:** An indirect quotation describes what a person said or wrote, but it does not use the person's exact words. The word *that* often introduces an indirect quotation. An indirect quotation is not enclosed in quotation marks.

> My mother always said that I shouldn't talk to strangers.

### Titles

**H-2**   Enclose the titles of these shorter works in quotation marks:

— chapter titles in books      — short poems
— magazine or newspaper articles      — songs
— short stories      — lectures

> After all these years, "As Time Goes By" is still my favorite song.
>
> Her article, "Ten Ways to Improve Your Marriage," is in the current *Reader's Digest*.

**Note:** Titles of these longer works are not placed in quotation marks. In handwriting, they are underlined. In print, they are in italics.

— books      — long poems
— periodicals      — movies and TV shows
  (magazines and newspapers)    — plays

> We subscribe to *Newsweek*, but we buy the *Daily News* at the newsstand.
>
> My favorite movie is *The King and I*, but I have never read the book it was taken from, *Anna and the King of Siam*.

# I: Single Quotation Marks

**I**    Use single quotation marks (' ') to enclose a quotation or title within a quotation.

> "The mayor can't pretend that Clinton's financial crisis has nothing to do with him," said Councilor Lewis. "As Harry Truman said, 'The buck stops here.' "

> "No one ever sang 'Somewhere Over the Rainbow,' " Sally said, "the way Judy Garland did."

**Assignment:** In Part A of Story 1, there is a line over the first mark in each set of quotation marks and single quotation marks. Note the use of each set of quotation marks or single quotation marks. On the line, write the correct letter and number from the list above (H-1 through I).

Where single quotation marks are used, note two rules:

1. the rule from section H that tells why quotation marks are needed
2. the rule from section I that tells why single quotation marks rather than ordinary quotation marks are used.

(For example, if the title of an article within a quotation is enclosed in single quotation marks, write H-2, I.)

### Story 1: Part A

‾"Take everything you hear about nutrition with a grain of salt," a noted nutritionist told a Clinton audience last night.

‾"But not too much salt," Harvey Kaplan added. ‾"It's not good for you." Kaplan, who writes the syndicated column ‾"Better Eating for Better Health," was speaking as part of a lecture series on health sponsored by Clinton Hospital.

‾"Twenty years ago," Kaplan said, ‾"nutritionists told you, ‾'Eat more meat, and cut down on starches.' Now we're learning that whole grains are important in a balanced diet and that too much meat can be dangerous."

Kaplan stressed the importance of a balanced diet. ‾"There are no miracle foods," he said. ‾"If you eat nothing but broccoli, you won't be any healthier than if you eat nothing but potato chips."

Edit Part B of Story 1 for internal punctuation according to rules A-1 through I. Insert internal punctuation where needed. Delete or change punctuation marks that are wrong. Use the proofreader's mark ( ℓ ) to delete punctuation marks ("John" Doe).

## Story 1: Part B

The columnist said that American's worst bad habit in eating is their taste for fast foods. He explained, That doesn't mean you should never go to McDonald's. I enjoy a Big Mac myself once in a while. But if thats your dinner every day, you're not eating right."

He also noted that eating habits formed in childhood often last a lifetime. "In the long run, he said, taking candy from a baby may be the biggest favor you could do for the kid.'

After his speech, Kaplan autographed copies of his latest book, "The Sensible Eating Guide," published last month by Emerald Books.

# J: Using Quotation Marks with Other Punctuation

Quotation marks often come next to a comma or an end punctuation mark in a sentence. The following rules tell how to use quotation marks with these other punctuation marks. The rules apply to single quotation marks as well.

**J-1**    Use a comma to set off a direct quotation from words like *she said*.

> "You were going 80 miles an hour," the policeman said.
> According to the Declaration of Independence, "All men are created equal."
> "Come with me," he told her, "and I will make you happy."

**J-2**    If a quoted question or exclamation comes at the beginning of a sentence, use a question mark (?) or an exclamation point (!) to set it off, not a comma.

> "Would you like squash or peas?" the waitress asked.
> "Unbelievable!" she burst out.

**J-3**    Commas and periods always go *inside* the quotation marks at the end of a quotation.

> "Listen carefully," she whispered.
> The mayor admitted, "Unless we get more state aid this year, property taxes will have to be raised."

**J-4**    Question marks and exclamation points go inside the quotation marks if the quotation itself is a question or exclamation.

> Judy asked, "Are you glad?"

*Are you glad?* is a question. Therefore, the question mark is part of the quotation, and it goes inside the quotation marks.

**J-5**    Question marks and exclamation points go outside the quotation marks if the sentence as a whole is a question or exclamation.

> Did she say, "I am going home"?

The quotation *"I am going home"* is a statement. The sentence as a whole is a question. Thus, the question mark goes outside the quotation marks.

**Assignment:** In Part A of Story 2, lines have been inserted above some internal punctuation marks. On each line, note the use of the punctuation mark. Write the letter and number of the rule, from A-1 through I. Where quotation marks are used along with other punctuation, also note the rule or rules from section J (J-1 through J-5). The first one is done for you.

### Story 2: Part A

Author Jean McNair last night brought back memories of the Great
<u>A-7</u>
Depression, which she said struck Clinton harder than most other parts of the country.

"People sometimes romanticize the Depression," the Clinton-born author told the Historical Society. "In Clinton, there was nothing romantic about it: the 1930s were hard times for almost everybody."

An article by McNair in this month's *Saturday Evening Post*, "We Never Lost Hope," describes what it was like to be a child in the Depression.

McNair's father was jobless for three years during the 1930s. Her family lived in the south end of Clinton. At that time, it was called the Swamp.

Part B of Story 2 has quotation marks around direct quotations but no other internal punctuation marks. Insert internal punctuation where needed according to the rules A-1 through J-5.

### Story 2: Part B

"It wasnt really a swamp of course" McNair told the Clinton Historical Society. "It was as dry as any other part of the state. I think people just called it the Swamp because the word sounded grubby."

According to McNair the south end "wasnt the worst part of town." She added that "the real down and outs lived in the east end."

In her view two factors made the Depression in Clinton "particularly hard." They were the closing of the Clinton Milling Company and "the collapse of farming which meant that nobody had any money to spend in the stores."

Edit Part C of Story 2 for internal punctuation according to rules A-1 through J-5. Insert internal punctuation where needed. Delete or change any punctuation marks that are wrong.

### Story 2: Part C

Two of McNairs books': "Far from the Towers" and "No One Called Us Poor" are about her childhood in Clinton during the 1930s.

"Even though life was hard" she told last nights meeting—"I still have fond memories of Clinton. The other day I heard a song on the radio called The Town I Loved So Well. I said to myself, "For me, thats Clinton." "

She asked the audience; "How many of you would have the same reaction to that song, 'The Town I Loved So Well?' And how many of you ask yourselves, as I do, 'Would I really have wanted to grow up anywhere else' "?

McNair has lived in New-York-City for the last 35 year's. Her sister and brother in law, Roberta and Daniel Marshall are residents of Mill Street in Clinton.

# — Part 3 —

# Parts of Speech

In a sentence, each word has a job to do. These jobs are given names just as employees of a company are given job titles. The job titles assigned to words are called parts of speech.

In the next seven chapters, we will discuss the functions of the parts of speech. We will look at the eight parts of speech in this order:

A. Nouns
B. Verbs
C. Prepositions
D. Pronouns
E. Modifiers (Adjectives and Adverbs)
F. Conjunctions
G. Interjections

# 9. Nouns

A noun names a person, place, thing, or idea. Some examples are *Ed, Ohio, truck*, and *freedom*. In the following sentences, the nouns are underlined:

> The <u>minister</u> delivered a <u>sermon</u> about <u>sin</u>.
> The <u>people</u> who lived in the green <u>house</u> moved to <u>Chicago</u>.
> The <u>noises</u> that <u>Melissa</u> scratches out of the <u>violin</u> don't sound like <u>music</u>.

Nouns provide the "cast of characters" for a sentence. One of their roles is to tell who or what is doing the action in the sentence—in other words, to be the subject of the sentence. The subjects of the sentences above are *minister, people*, and *noises*.

Nouns play other roles as well. They tell whom or what the action is done to, who is affected by it, what is causing it.

## Common and Proper Nouns

A common noun is one that can stand for *any* person, place, or thing that it names. Examples are *woman, city*, and *school*.

A proper noun is one that names a specific person, place, or thing. Examples are *Sally Ride, San Francisco*, and *Howe Junior College*.

Proper nouns begin with a capital letter. The rules you learned for capitalizing words in chapter 2 will help you with proper nouns.

## Possessive Forms of Nouns

Nouns show ownership, or possession, of something by adding the ending *-'s* or *-s'*. Examples are *Bob's car, the Smiths' house, the men's room*. The rules you learned for using the apostrophe in chapter 7 will help you use possessive forms of nouns correctly.

## Singular and Plural

Nouns can be singular (one) or plural (more than one). The nouns in the following sentence are singular:

> While crossing the <u>street</u>, <u>William</u> was almost hit by a <u>bus</u>.

The nouns in the following sentences are plural:

> <u>Fields</u> of <u>daisies</u> stretched before her <u>eyes</u>.
> The <u>Johnsons</u> have three <u>children</u>.

**Regular plurals.** Most plural nouns are formed by adding *-s* or *-es* to the singular form. These are some examples:

| Singular | Plural | Singular | Plural |
|----------|--------|----------|--------|
| track | tracks | branch | branches |
| tree | trees | ash | ashes |
| book | books | boss | bosses |
| face | faces | box | boxes |
| rose | roses | quiz | quizzes |
| | | potato | potatoes |
| | | baby | babies |

Some nouns that end in *lf* or a long vowel and *f* change *f* to *v* and then add *-es*. Here are some examples:

| Singular | Plural | Singular | Plural |
|----------|--------|----------|--------|
| calf | calves | leaf | leaves |
| half | halves | loaf | loaves |
| shelf | shelves | knife | knives |
| | | thief | thieves |

**Irregular plurals.** A few nouns form their plurals in other ways:

| Singular | Plural | Singular | Plural |
|----------|--------|----------|--------|
| person | people | foot | feet |
| man | men | tooth | teeth |
| woman | women | goose | geese |
| child | children | mouse | mice |
| ox | oxen | louse | lice |

There are also a few words, such as *fish, moose,* and *sheep,* that are the same in the singular and the plural.

**Assignment:** In Story 1, underline all nouns. The first one is done for you.

### Story 1

A local <u>youth</u> has been charged with possession of marijuana after being arrested by police. The name of the youth was not released because he is a juvenile.

An ounce of the drug was found in the lining of the youth's coat, police said. The arrest was the third on charges related to drugs in Clinton in the last month.

The youth was released on bail and will be brought to trial in juvenile court.

In Part A of Story 2, there is a box after each noun. Mark **S** in the box if the noun is singular and **P** if the noun is plural. The first one is done for you.

### Story 2: Part A

Traditional methods ☐P of farming ☐ will be the theme ☐ of the annual Open House ☐ at the Model Farm ☐ on Highway ☐ 23.

Visitors ☐ to the event ☐ will be able to see demonstrations ☐ of how farmers ☐ around Clinton ☐ tended their fields ☐ 100 years ☐ ago.

Harvesting ☐ with the scythe ☐ and using ☐ a plow ☐ drawn by oxen ☐ will be among the skills ☐ demonstrated.

In Part B of Story 2, all nouns are underlined and given in the singular form. If the noun should be plural, cross out the singular form, and write in the correct plural form above it. If the noun should be singular, leave it as it is. The first one is done for you.

### Story 2: Part B

*Crafts*
~~Craft~~ that were practiced by rural woman will also be featured. Several woman dressed in costume of the period will show how to use a spinning wheel and a loom.

Antique quilt and braided rug will be displayed in the farmhouse that stands at the entrance to the farm.

For $5, visitor will be able to buy a meal featuring dish that were cooked in rural kitchen and made with ingredient that were produced on farm in the area.

Another attraction will be the petting zoo, where child will be able to look at, touch, and feed tame animal and bird.

In Part C of Story 2, there are errors in the use of singular and plural nouns. Nouns may be singular when they should be plural or plural when they should be singular, or incorrect plural forms may be used. Edit the story to correct these errors. (The marks to use in editing are shown in Instructions for Editing at the beginning of this book.)

### Story 2: Part C

Ducks, gooses, goats, and sheeps will be among the animals in the petting zoo. Each children will get one cupful of food for the animals as part of the price of admission.

Saturday night, visitors are invited to clap their hands and stamp their feets to the lively music of the Country Bumpkins at the Old-Fashioned Barn Dance.

Admission to the Open House is $4 for men and woman and $2 for children.

# 10. Verbs

## Words That Show Action or Being

**Action verbs.** A verb is usually a word that expresses action. *Hit, crash, swim*, and *learn* are all action verbs. The action verbs are underlined in the following sentences:

Clinton residents gave more than $100,000 to the Community Chest last year.

The window rattles whenever the wind blows.

Jack Tupper hit two home runs as the Clinton Tigers won their fourth game in a row.

**Linking verbs.** Some verbs link the subject to the rest of the sentence. These verbs do not express action. They are called linking verbs.

The most common linking verb is the verb *be*. It has a variety of forms:

| | | | | |
|---|---|---|---|---|
| am | was | will be | could be | has been |
| is | were | | would be | have been |
| are | | | should be | |

Other examples of linking verbs are:

| | | | |
|---|---|---|---|
| become | seem | grow | feel |
| | look | | taste |
| | appear | | smell |

The underlined verbs in the following sentences are all linking verbs:

We were in Montreal on our last trip to Canada.
His daughter became an engineer.
She grew old gracefully.
His cold seems a little better today.
The kitchen smells good.

**Verb phrases.** Sometimes a verb is made up of more than one word. Then it is known as a verb phrase. A verb phrase consists of a main verb and one or more helping verbs. The most common helping verbs are forms of the verb *be*. Other common helping verbs are:

| | | | | | |
|---|---|---|---|---|---|
| has | do | can | may | will | could |
| have | does | must | might | shall | would |
| | did | | | | should |

The following sentences contain verb phrases. The helping verbs are underlined once and the main verbs are underlined twice.

>He <u>might</u> <u>have</u> <u>won</u> the state championship if he <u>had</u> <u>trained</u> more diligently.

>She <u>has</u> <u>come</u> a long way and <u>should</u> <u>reach</u> her potential within the next few years.

>By the end of the year, the company's profit <u>will</u> <u>have</u> <u>fallen</u>, but its debt <u>will</u> <u>have</u> <u>doubled</u>.

**Assignment:** In Story 1, there is a box after each verb. Put an **A** in the box if the verb is an action verb and an **L** if it is a linking verb. The first one is done for you.

### Story 1

Police arrested ☐A an elderly man at the corner of Main and Water streets yesterday.

The man appeared ☐ drunk and acted ☐ in a disorderly manner. Police identified ☐ him as Harold Aitken, 66, of South Main Street.

Aitken attracted ☐ the attention of police when he shouted ☐ at passersby. He was ☐ unshaven and looked ☐ unkempt, police said. ☐

Police later released ☐ the man without charge.

In Story 2, underline all verb phrases. The first one is done for you.

### Story 2

Main Street <u>will be closed</u> to traffic between Water Street and Chestnut Street tomorrow. Road crews will be repairing the damage that was done by cold weather this past winter.

The Clinton Maintenance Department is asking motorists to use Hill Street while Main Street is closed.

A spokesman for the department said he was hoping that the work would be finished by sundown.

# Subject-Verb Agreement

Verbs sometimes take different forms depending on what the subject is. A subject can either be singular (one) or plural (more than one).

In addition, a subject can be first, second, or third person. The first person is the person speaking (*I* or *we*), the second person is the person being spoken to (*you*), and the third person is another person or thing being spoken about (*he, she, it,* or *they*). In a chart, it looks like this:

|  | **Singular** | **Plural** |
|---|---|---|
| **First person** | I do | we do |
| **Second person** | you do | you do |
| **Third person** | he does<br>she does<br>it does | they do |

**Third person singular.** Note that only the third person singular changes. The form of the verb stays the same in all the other boxes. This form is the base from which other forms of the verb are made.

For most verbs, the third person singular is formed by adding *-s* or *-es* to the base:

|  | **Singular** | **Plural** |
|---|---|---|
| **First person** | I dance | we dance |
| **Second person** | you dance | you dance |
| **Third person** | he dances<br>she dances<br>it dances | they dance |

All nouns are third person. Therefore, when the subject is a singular noun, the verb takes the *-s* or *-es* form. When the subject is a plural noun, the verb remains in the base form.

> Ann dances more smoothly since her Arthur Murray course.
>
> The Rockettes dance at Radio City Music Hall.
>
> Jason does his homework every night.
>
> Parrots talk by imitating human sounds.

**The verb _have_.** The verb _have_ makes the third person singular from the base in a slightly different way from other verbs:

|  | Singular | Plural |
|---|---|---|
| **First person** | I have | we have |
| **Second person** | you have | you have |
| **Third person** | he has<br>she has<br>it has | they have |

Use _has_ with all singular nouns and with _he, she,_ or _it._ Use _have_ with everything else. Note that a compound subject joined by _and_ is plural.

Mr. Miller has a collection of Kennedy half dollars.

He and his wife also have a collection of road maps.

**The verb _be_.** The verb _be_ is formed in a completely different way:

|  | Singular | Plural |
|---|---|---|
| **First person** | I am | we are |
| **Second person** | you are | you are |
| **Third person** | he is<br>she is<br>it is | they are |

Use _am_ only after _I._ Use _is_ with all singular nouns and with _he, she,_ or _it._ Use _are_ with everything else. Again, note that a compound subject joined by _and_ is plural.

The chief of police is appointed by the mayor, but the sheriff is elected.

I am exhausted.

You and I are on duty this week.

Voters are eager for the election; they are tired of the candidates' TV commercials.

**Assignment:** In Part A of Story 3, all verbs are underlined and given in the base form. If this is not the correct form, cross out the base form, and write in the correct form above it. If it is the correct form, leave it as it is. The first one is done for you.

## Story 3: Part A

As the economic boom ~~continue~~ *continues*, all signs point to a rally in the stock market.

"It look like a good time for an investment in stocks," say Woodrow Blakeney, a New York market analyst. "A rising stock market be almost certain."

Blakeney have confidence that the economy's foundations be solid. "I be an optimist about the economy," he add.

In Part B of Story 3, some verbs are not in the correct form. Edit the story to correct these errors. (The marks to use in editing are shown in Instructions for Editing at the beginning of this book.) The first one is done for you.

## Story 3: Part B

Blakeney argue*s* that high-technology stocks are the best investment: "I believes that the basis of our future are high technology."

Nowadays, many investors stay away from manufacturing stocks such as General Motors and U.S. Steel. Blakeney think that this is a mistake.

"Manufacturing have its problems," he admits. He insists, however, that "these problems is not as serious as some people thinks."

# Verb Tenses

The tense of a verb indicates the time of the action. There are three main tenses: present, future, and past.

**Present tense.** The present tense indicates something that is true now or that happens regularly. The verbs given in all of the charts above (such as *I dance, he dances*) are the forms of the simple present tense. The underlined verbs in the following sentences are in the simple present tense:

> She always <u>walks</u> to work.
> That old building <u>is</u> a fire hazard.
> We <u>want</u> shorter hours and higher wages.

**Future tense.** The future tense indicates something that will happen at some time in the future. The underlined verbs in the following sentences are in the future tense:

> If you don't hurry, you <u>will miss</u> the bus.
> Mayor Johnson <u>will announce</u> his candidacy for re-election tomorrow.
> A hundred years from now, people <u>will build</u> cities on the moon.

The future tense is formed by putting the helping verb *will* before the verb base. The future tense remains the same no matter what the subject is.

**Past tense.** The past tense indicates something that has already happened. The underlined verbs in the following sentences are in the past tense:

> I just <u>woke</u> up.
> Governor Ryan <u>opened</u> the new state office building yesterday.

For all verbs except *be*, the form of the past tense remains the same no matter what the subject is. The verb *be* has two forms of the past tense, *was* and *were*.

|  | Singular | Plural |
|---|---|---|
| **First person** | I was | we were |
| **Second person** | you were | you were |
| **Third person** | he was<br>she was<br>it was | they were |

> You <u>were</u> in fourth grade when I <u>was</u> in third grade.
> The Romans <u>were</u> the masters of the ancient world.

Most verbs form the past tense by adding *-d* or *-ed* to the base. Here are some examples:

| **Base** | **Past Tense** |
|---|---|
| talk | talked |
| dance | danced |
| stop | stopped |
| hurry | hurried |

Some verbs change in a different way to form the past tense. You will learn more about them in the next section.

# Other Forms of Verbs

Verbs have other forms that have other uses.

**Infinitives.** The infinitive is *to* plus the base form of the verb.

> I would like <u>to win</u> the state lottery.
> My boss asked me <u>to work</u> overtime.

**The -*ing* form.** The ending -*ing* can be added to the base (for example, *go, going*). This form can be used together with a form of *be* as its helping verb.

> I don't know what he <u>is talking</u> about.
> We <u>were dancing</u> when the police came.

**The past participle.** The past participle is the form of the verb used with the helping verbs *has, have,* and *had.*

> I <u>have lived</u> here for 20 years.
> Jack <u>has fallen</u> asleep in every movie he <u>has gone</u> to.
> We <u>had finished</u> the job an hour before quitting time.

The past participle can also be used after *be* to form passive verbs.

> This part of Maryland <u>is called</u> the Eastern Shore.
> The boy <u>was found</u> in the forest after a lengthy search by state police.

The past participle of most verbs is formed by adding -*d* or -*ed* to the base, the same as the past tense.

| Base | Past Tense | Past Participle |
|------|------------|-----------------|
| I dance | I danced | I have danced |
| We manage | We managed | We have managed |
| You work | You worked | You have worked |
| They hurry | They hurried | They have hurried |

**Regular and irregular verbs.** Verbs that form both the past tense and past participle by adding -*d* or -*ed* are called regular verbs. Some verbs form the past tense and past participle in different ways. These verbs are called irregular verbs.

> By hitting four home runs in one game, he <u>broke</u> a team record.
> The boss fired her because she <u>wore</u> jeans to work.
> The clouds <u>have begun</u> to lift.
> This intersection <u>is known</u> to be the most dangerous in Clinton.

A few irregular verbs are the same in all three forms—base, past tense, and past participle. Some examples are:

| | | | | |
|------|------|------|------|------|
| cost | hit | let | quit | shut |
| cut | hurt | put | set | split |

The following chart shows the base, past tense, and past participle of other common irregular verbs.

# Irregular Verbs

| Base Form | Past Tense | Past Participle |
|---|---|---|
| (We) become | (We) became | (We have) become |
| begin | began | begun |
| bite | bit | bitten |
| break | broke | broken |
| bring | brought | brought |
| buy | bought | bought |
| choose | chose | chosen |
| come | came | come |
| do | did | done |
| drink | drank | drunk |
| drive | drove | driven |
| eat | ate | eaten |
| fall | fell | fallen |
| feel | felt | felt |
| find | found | found |
| fly | flew | flown |
| get | got | got *or* gotten |
| give | gave | given |
| go | went | gone |
| grow | grew | grown |
| hear | heard | heard |
| keep | kept | kept |
| know | knew | known |
| lead | led | led |
| make | made | made |
| mean | meant | meant |
| read | read | read |
| ride | rode | ridden |
| run | ran | run |
| say | said | said |
| see | saw | seen |
| sell | sold | sold |
| send | sent | sent |
| sleep | slept | slept |
| spend | spent | spent |
| speak | spoke | spoken |
| stick | stuck | stuck |
| take | took | taken |
| teach | taught | taught |
| tell | told | told |
| think | thought | thought |
| throw | threw | thrown |
| wear | wore | worn |
| win | won | won |
| write | wrote | written |

**Assignment:** In Story 4, the verbs in parentheses are in the base form. They should be in the past tense or past participle. Cross out the base form, and write the correct form above it. The first one is done for you.

### Story 4

*received*

Eighteen students (receive) their diplomas last night at the annual Clinton Adult Learning Center graduation.

The students all (pass) their GED exams after having (take) a course of study equivalent to high school.

School Committee Chairman Elizabeth Aird (give) the students their diplomas. "We in the school system have (take) much pride in the growth of the Adult Learning Center," she (tell) them.

Anthony Jelinek of Clinton, who has (study) at the center since last September, (speak) for the graduates. "When we (begin)," he (say), "some of us (think) we had (bite) off more than we could chew. But we (stick) to it. Now we can look back and say, 'We (do) it.' "

The guest speaker (be) Elliott Woodsworth, Clinton's representative in the state legislature. Woodsworth (get) his law degree after he (spend) 10 years studying at night and working in the daytime. He (speak) about his own experiences as an adult student. He (say) these experiences (make) him appreciate "the commitment and hard work you have (bring) to your studies."

Paul Thatcher, director of Howe Junior College, (present) a $50 scholarship to Eugene Romanow of Clinton. Romanow's sister, Janet McGee, (win) the same scholarship three years ago. She has since (become) a computer programmer after receiving an associate's degree at Howe.

In Part A of Story 5, there is a box after each verb. Write **PR** in the box if the verb is in the present tense, **PA** if it is in the past tense, and **F** if it is in the future tense. The first one is done for you.

### Story 5: Part A

The Clinton Tigers won $\boxed{PA}$ the county baseball championship yesterday when they defeated $\boxed{\phantom{PA}}$ the Milford Marauders 4-3 in 11 innings.

Jim Turner earned $\boxed{\phantom{PA}}$ the "Player of the Game" award when he hit $\boxed{\phantom{PA}}$ a double in the eleventh inning. The double scored $\boxed{\phantom{PA}}$ Don Bracken from first base, broke $\boxed{\phantom{PA}}$ a 3-3 tie, and won $\boxed{\phantom{PA}}$ the game for the Tigers.

The victory means $\boxed{\phantom{PA}}$ that the Tigers will play $\boxed{\phantom{PA}}$ in the state championships that will begin $\boxed{\phantom{PA}}$ next Saturday in Springfield.

In Part B of Story 5, all verbs are underlined and given in the base form. Consider both the subject of the verb and the tense that the verb should be. If the base form is not the correct form, cross it out, and write in the correct form above it. The first one is done for you.

### Story 5: Part B

"This year's Tigers ~~be~~ *are* the best ever," <u>say</u> a happy Coach Steve Borden after the game. "We <u>be</u> tough in the state championships."

In next week's opening round, the Tigers <u>face</u> the Johnstown Bears, who <u>win</u> the championship of Washington County with a 7-1 record.

Chuck Lang, who <u>win</u> three games for the Tigers in county play, <u>be</u> the starting pitcher against Johnstown. Lang <u>be</u> a left-hander whose best pitch <u>be</u> a fastball.

In Part C of Story 5, some verbs are not in the correct form. Edit the story to correct each of these errors. Take into account both the subject of the verb and the tense that the verb should be. (The marks to use in editing are shown in Instructions for Editing at the beginning of this book.) The first one is done for you.

### Story 5: Part C

Turner ~~hits~~ _hit_ a two-run homer and a single in yesterday's game in addition to his game-winning double. He were also outstanding in the field as he throw out three Marauder runners.

Ron Bowell will drive in the other Clinton run when he hit a single in the ninth inning and scores Carl Abbott. The run tied the game at 3-3 and force it into extra innings.

The Tigers celebrated their victory with a parade down Main Street tomorrow. Before yesterday's win, the Tigers last capture the county championship 11 years ago.

# 11. Prepositions

A preposition shows how the words that follow it are related to the rest of the sentence.

> Firemen rushed <u>to</u> the burning house.
>
> A baby was crying <u>in</u> the burning house.

The relationship of the rushing firemen to the burning house is different from the relationship of the crying baby to that house. These different relationships are shown by using two different prepositions, *to* and *in*.

Prepositions are usually "little words." The following are some common prepositions:

| | | | | | |
|---|---|---|---|---|---|
| above | before | by | in | on | under |
| across | behind | down | into | out | up |
| after | below | during | like | over | upon |
| among | beside | except | near | through | with |
| at | between | for | of | to | without |
| | but | from | off | toward | |

(*But* is a preposition only when it means *except*.)

In the following sentences, the prepositions are underlined.

> No one <u>but</u> Rich Little can talk <u>like</u> Jimmy Stewart.
>
> The battalion struck <u>under</u> the cover <u>of</u> darkness, just <u>before</u> dawn.
>
> New Hampshire is located north <u>of</u> Massachusetts, <u>between</u> Vermont and Maine.
>
> She rushed <u>down</u> the stairs, <u>out</u> the door, and <u>into</u> the waiting taxi.

**Assignment:** In Part A of Story 1, circle all of the prepositions. The first one is done for you.

### Story 1: Part A

A winter storm swept (across) the plains states yesterday. It buried the area under 18 inches of snow. Parts of Montana, South Dakota, and Iowa were left without electric power.

The storm crossed the border from Canada after bringing snow and cold temperatures to the Canadian prairies.

No deaths or injuries were attributed to the storm. Many motorists spent the night in motels, however, when their cars got stuck on snow-covered roads.

In Part B of Story 1, each blank indicates a place where a preposition should be. For each blank, choose a preposition from the above list and write it in the blank. Be sure that each sentence and the story as a whole make sense. The prepositions in the list may be used more than once. The first blank is filled in for you.

## Story 1: Part B

A winter storm warning is __*in*__ effect today _____ northern Michigan _____ southern Tennessee, as the storm moves slowly _____ the east.

The storm is expected to bring snow _____ the eastern seaboard tomorrow _____ going out _____ sea.

_____ Montana, crews are working to restore electric power _____ communities left _____ the dark _____ the storm. Electrical service was back _____ normal _____ 6 a.m. today _____ South Dakota and Iowa.

In Part C of Story 1, some sentences do not make sense because the wrong prepositions have been used. Edit the story to correct these errors. (The marks to use in editing are shown in Instructions for Editing at the beginning of this book.) The first one is done for you.

## Story 1: Part C

Authorities ~~behind~~ *in* Nebraska closed parts of Interstate 80 to allow tow trucks to remove stalled cars under the road. Motorists are asked to stay on all roads unless their trip is an emergency.

This was the fourth major storm toward the season in the plains states, making it the area's worst winter before 20 years. A low-pressure system now forming after the Canadian Arctic may bring more snow to the area by Friday.

Authorities estimate the cost by cleaning up the snow from yesterday's storm at $2 million.

# 12. Pronouns

A common definition of a pronoun is "a word that takes the place of a noun." Sometimes this is easy to see, as in the example below.

> Alice does not know what shift <u>she</u> will be working next week.

But it is not always easy to use this definition to tell if a word is a pronoun or a noun. The easiest thing to do is just to learn the pronouns. There are not many, and they belong to just a few groups, so learning them is not difficult.

## Personal Pronouns

The most commonly used pronouns are called personal pronouns. They have different forms for different uses. These forms are shown in the chart below.

**Singular and plural.** First, look at the two groups going across—singular and plural. The singular form is used for one. The plural form is used for two or more.

|  | **Subjective** | **Objective** | **Possessive** |
|---|---|---|---|
| **Singular** | I | me | my, mine |
|  | you | you | your, yours |
|  | he | him | his |
|  | she | her | her, hers |
|  | it | it | its |
| **Plural** | we | us | our, ours |
|  | you | you | your, yours |
|  | they | them | their, theirs |

Next, look at the three columns going down—subjective, objective, and possessive. These forms have different uses in sentences. In short, subjective forms are used as subjects. Objective forms are used as objects. And possessive forms are used to show that someone owns something. More specific rules follow.

**Subjective pronouns** have two uses:

**Subj-1**   Use a subjective pronoun as the subject of a sentence or clause.

> <u>They</u> scored 22 points in the fourth quarter.
> <u>He</u> sold the quilt that <u>she</u> had made for $275.
> <u>He</u> and <u>I</u> have been friends for many years.

**Subj-2**  Use a subjective pronoun after any form of the verb *be* when you are writing or speaking formally.

It was not I who killed Cock Robin; it was he.

Franklin D. Roosevelt was a great president. It was he who led the country during the Second World War.

Mrs. McDougall will handle your loan application. I believe it was she who spoke to you about it last week.

**Note:** Informally, objective pronouns are often used after the verb *be*:

I didn't write on the wall; it was him.
Are you looking for Margie? That's her over there.

For another example of formal and informal usage, think of the telephone. On a business phone, if the caller asks, "May I speak to (your name)?" you would answer, "This is he" or "This is she."

But suppose you are phoning your own home. You say "Hello." The member of your family who answers doesn't recognize your voice and asks, "Who's calling, please?" You answer, "It's me."

**Objective pronouns** have three uses:

**Obj-1**  Use an objective pronoun after an action verb to indicate the person or thing the action was done to.

They beat us by six points.
He kissed her on the cheek.

**Obj-2**  Use an objective pronoun after a preposition.

She brought the book to me.
He ran after them as fast as he could.

**Obj-3**  Use an objective pronoun as an indirect object, when the preposition *to* or *for* is understood but not expressed.

Sue gave him a birthday present.
(Sue gave a birthday present to him.)

If you're going to the store, get me some razor blades.
(If you're going to the store, get some razor blades for me.)

**Possessive pronouns** have two forms. Use the first form in the chart (*my, your,* etc.) when the pronoun comes just before the thing that is owned. Otherwise, use the second form (*mine, yours,* etc.).

Possessive pronouns have two uses:

**Poss-1**  Use a possessive pronoun to show ownership.

Her book was found on the bus.
The book that was found on the bus was hers.

**Poss-2**  Use a possessive pronoun before a verb that has *-ing* added to it and is used as a noun.

We were all happy about his getting a job.
I know my being gone will be hard for you.

**Pronouns in compound subjects and objects.** When a pronoun is part of a compound like *John and I*, it is sometimes hard to decide which form of the pronoun to use. In such cases, mentally leave out the other half of the compound, and find the rule that applies to the pronoun.

**Example 1:**     The vase is a present from Mary and (I, me).

Mentally leave out *Mary*:

> The vase is a present from . . . me.
> (objective pronoun after preposition)

Therefore:     The vase is a present from Mary and me.

**Example 2:**     The party really got started after you and (she, her) went home.

Mentally leave out *you*:

> The party really got started after . . . she went home.
> (subjective pronoun as subject of dependent clause)

Therefore:     The party really got started after you and she went home.

**Note:** It is considered polite to put yourself last in a compound subject or object. Thus, it is better to say *He and I liked it* than *I and he liked it.*

**We or us + a noun.** The pronouns *we* and *us* can be followed by a noun, such as *we men* or *us men*. The trick is in knowing whether to use *we* or *us*.

> (We, Us) men did the cooking for the dinner.
> Several of the women told (we, us) men that it was delicious.

To decide whether *we* or *us* is correct, mentally leave out the noun that follows it.

> We . . . did the cooking for the dinner.
> Several of the women told us . . . that it was delicious.

Thus:

> We men did the cooking for the dinner.
> Several of the women told us men that it was delicious.

**The pronoun *its* and the contraction *it's*.** Remember that *its* without an apostrophe is the possessive form of the pronoun *it*. The word *it's* with an apostrophe is a contraction of *it is* or *it has*.

> In the accident, my car's left front fender was smashed, and its radiator was badly damaged.

> It's [It is] easier to give advice than to take it.

> It's [It has] been a long time since I have seen her.

**Comparisons with *than* and *as . . . as.*** Using pronouns in comparisons made with *than* or *as . . . as* can be tricky.

> John is taller than (I, me).
> Alice sings as well as (I, me).

*Than* and *as* look like prepositions. But they are not. They are conjunctions (joining words). They join a clause or phrase to the rest of the sentence. But often words in the clause or phrase are left out. If you put those words back in, it is easier to see which form of the pronoun to use.

> He is taller than I am.
> He is taller than I.
>
> She sings as well as I do.
> She sings as well as I.

**Assignment:** In Part A of Story 1, there is a box after each pronoun. Write **S** in the box if the pronoun is subjective, **O** if it is objective, and **P** if it is possessive. The first one is done for you.

### Story 1: Part A

The Clinton Little Theater Group staged its P best production yet last night when it ☐ presented Tennessee Williams's play *The Glass Menagerie.*

Williams wrote the play more than 40 years ago, but last night's production made it ☐ seem fresh and modern.

Most of the credit for its ☐ success belongs to the cast—especially to Pearl Wilson, who gave her ☐ best performance to date. Wilson played Laura, the main character in the play. She ☐ gave the character a depth of feeling that I ☐ have rarely seen on the local stage.

In Part B of Story 1, all pronouns are underlined and given in the subjective form. Whenever this is not the correct form, cross out the subjective form, and write the correct form above it. The first one is done for you.

### Story 1: Part B

Robert Oliver also turned in <u>he</u> *his* best performance yet as <u>she</u> brother, Tom. Perhaps <u>he</u> improvement is a result of <u>he</u> having studied for six months at a drama school in New York.

Lillian Kane appeared as <u>they</u> proud mother, Amanda. <u>She</u>, too, played <u>she</u> character with strength and conviction. The best lines in the play are <u>she</u>, and <u>she</u> delivered <u>they</u> well.

In Part C of Story 1, some pronouns are not in the correct form. Edit the story to correct these errors. (The marks to use in editing are shown in Instructions for Editing at the beginning of this book.) The first error is corrected for you.

## Story 1: Part C

As portrayed by Kane, Amanda made it clear that it was ~~her~~ *she* who had turned her daughter into a wallflower and her son into a cynic. The exchanges between Wilson and she were fascinating to watch.

Paul Jolliffe as the gentleman caller did not have the same polish as the other members of the cast. He did have some fine moments, however. Him drawing Laura out of her shyness while him and her explored their past was the highlight of his performance.

Us Clinton theater-goers have waited a long time for a production of this quality. Now that it has come, the pleasure is our.

Congratulations to the Clinton Little Theater Group. Clinton is lucky to have performers as good as them.

# Reflexive Pronouns

Reflexive pronouns are made up of a personal pronoun and *self* or *selves*. The reflexive pronouns are:

| **Singular** | **Plural** |
|---|---|
| myself | ourselves |
| yourself | yourselves |
| himself | themselves |
| herself | |
| itself | |

**Used to "reflect" action.** A reflexive pronoun is used after a verb to show that the action is "reflected" back on the subject:

> I hurt <u>myself</u>.  It turns <u>itself</u> on and off.
> He killed <u>himself</u>.  They enjoyed <u>themselves</u>.

A reflexive pronoun can also be used after a preposition:

> She lives by <u>herself</u>.
> He got maple syrup all over <u>himself</u>.

The pronoun *you* can be either singular or plural. Use the reflexive pronoun *yourself* when *you* is singular and *yourselves* when *you* is plural:

> Jimmy, did you hurt <u>yourself</u>?
> You should all be ashamed of <u>yourselves</u>.

**Used for emphasis.** The reflexive pronouns are also used for emphasis:

> If no one else will do it, I will do it <u>myself</u>.
> Elvis Presley <u>himself</u> once slept in this bed.

**Forms to avoid.** Do not use *hisself* or *theirselves*. The correct forms are *himself* and *themselves*.

# Demonstrative Pronouns

A demonstrative pronoun points out a particular person or thing. The demonstrative pronouns are shown in the chart below.

| Singular | Plural | |
|----------|--------|---|
| this | these | (*This* and *these* refer to things near the speaker.) |
| that | those | (*That* and *those* refer to things farther away from the speaker.) |

The demonstrative pronouns are underlined in the following sentences.

> <u>This</u> is my pen; yours is in your coat pocket.
> <u>That</u> is not a good idea.
> <u>Those</u> are the highest mountains I have ever seen.

**Used with *kind, type,* and *sort*.** Remember that *this* and *that* are singular. With them, use the singular form: *kind, type,* and *sort.*

*These* and *those* are plural. With them, use the plural form with *-s.*

| Singular | | Plural | |
|----------|---|--------|---|
| this kind | that kind | these kinds | those kinds |
| this type | that type | these types | those types |
| this sort | that sort | these sorts | those sorts |

> I like <u>that</u> <u>kind</u> of movie best.
> I don't like <u>those</u> <u>kinds</u> of music.

**Forms to avoid.** Don't use *this here* or *that there* for *this* or *that.*

> (Wrong)   This here is a good restaurant.
> (Right)   <u>This</u> is a good restaurant.

Don't use *them* in front of a noun. Use *those* instead.

> (Wrong)   I don't like them boys.
> (Right)   I don't like <u>those</u> boys.

# Relative Pronouns

A relative pronoun is used to introduce a dependent clause. The relative pronouns are *who, which, that,* and *what.*

**Forms of relative pronouns.** *Who* has three forms: *who* (subjective), *whom* (objective), and *whose* (possessive).

*Who* refers only to people. *Which* and *what* refer to animals or things. *That* can refer to people, animals, or things.

In the following sentences, the relative pronouns are underlined:

> The woman whose house we are buying is a teacher.
> He knows what he wants.
> The only magazine that I read is *McCall's.*
> Labor Day, which falls on the first Monday in September, is celebrated with parades and picnics.

**When to use *who* and *whom*.** The rules for using *who* and *whom* are the same as for other subjective and objective pronouns. The thing to remember is that the correct form of *who* depends on how it is used in the dependent clause.

If you are in doubt about using *who* or *whom*, look at the dependent clause by itself. Change the word order to that of a normal sentence. Then substitute the correct form of a personal pronoun.

**Example 1:**    The man (who, whom) Jane had robbed took her to court.

The dependent clause is (*who, whom*) *Jane had robbed.* Change the word order, and substitute the personal pronoun that would stand for *man:*

> Jane had robbed him.
> (objective pronoun after action verb)

Therefore:    The man whom Jane had robbed took her to court.

**Example 2:**    People to (who, whom) the new tax law applies should be careful in filling out their tax returns.

The clause is *to (who, whom) the new tax law applies.* Change the word order, and substitute the pronoun that would stand for *people:*

> The new tax law applies to them.
> (objective pronoun after preposition)

Therefore:    People to whom the new tax law applies should be careful in filling out their tax returns.

After doing this a few times, you may not need to substitute a pronoun any more. Just changing the word order will probably be enough to tell you whether to use *who* or *whom.*

**Example 3:**    She knows (who, whom) I am.

The clause is (*who, whom*) *I am.* Change the word order:

> I am who.
> (subjective pronoun after a form of the verb be)

Therefore:    She knows who I am.

# Interrogative Pronouns

*What, which,* and the three forms of *who* are also used in questions. Then they are called interrogative pronouns.

What is your name?
Which do you like better, coffee or tea?
Who is that man?
To whom was the letter addressed?
Whose is that car parked in front of the fire hydrant?

**Assignment:** In Part A of Story 2, there is a box after each demonstrative, reflexive, or relative pronoun. Write **D** in the box if it is a demonstrative pronoun, **RF** if it is a reflexive pronoun, and **RL** if it is a relative pronoun.

### Story 2: Part A

People who ☐ do not know themselves ☐ do things that ☐ are not good for them. People who ☐ are more in tune with their own personalities are able to make better decisions. In today's "Ask Dr. Wintermeyer" column, you will get to know yourself ☐ a little better. That ☐ is the purpose of today's quiz.

Look carefully at the eight statements that ☐ follow. Give yourself ☐ 2 points for each one that ☐ you agree with, 1 point for each one about which ☐ you are not sure, and no points for each one that ☐ you disagree with.

1. Money, power, success—those ☐ are the important things in life.

In Part B of Story 2, wherever the word *demonstrative* appears in parentheses, cross it out, and write the correct demonstrative pronoun above it. Do the same for *reflexive* pronouns and *relative* pronouns. The first one is done for you.

### Story 2: Part B

     *who*
2. People (relative) don't work as hard as they can are just lazy.

3. People to (relative) happiness means more than money are just fooling (reflexive).

4. When I take a day off, I don't know (relative) to do with (reflexive).

5. There are many times when I am under a lot of pressure at work, but (demonstrative) are the situations in (relative) I am happiest.

In Part C of Story 2, there are errors in the use of demonstrative, reflexive, and relative pronouns. Edit the story to correct these errors. (The marks to use in editing are shown in Instructions for Editing at the beginning of this book.) The first one is done for you.

### Story 2: Part C

6. People are competitive—this ~~here~~ is a fact of human nature.

7. Retirement is the thing whom I dread most.

8. People whom are unable to stand stress are just sissies.

Add up your score to see what personality type you are. If you scored between 12 and 16, you are an achiever which will get ahead, but you may be slowly killing yourself with too much stress. If you scored between 6 and 11, you are a mixed personality type. This here is what most of us are. If you scored between 0 and 5, you are laid back. You won't make it in the rat race, but you won't burn yourselves out, either. You may live to be 100.

# Indefinite Pronouns

An indefinite pronoun refers to a person, place, thing, or idea in general. In the following sentences, the indefinite pronouns are underlined:

> Anything you can do will be appreciated.
> He blamed Clinton's rapid growth for many of its problems.
> None of the candidates has taken a position on the expressway issue.

It is not always clear whether a singular verb (such as *is, has, dances*) or a plural verb (such as *are, have, dance*) should be used after an indefinite pronoun. It is best just to learn the indefinite pronouns in groups—those that take a singular verb, those that take a plural verb, and those that can take either depending on how they are used.

| **Singular:** | each | anyone | anything | anybody | |
|---|---|---|---|---|---|
| | either | someone | something | somebody | |
| | neither | everyone | everything | everybody | |
| | other | no one | nothing | nobody | |
| | another | one | much | | |
| **Plural:** | both | few | many | several | |
| **Either:** | all | most | some | any | none |

In each of the following sentences, the indefinite pronoun is underlined once, and the verb is underlined twice:

> Neither of the plans is satisfactory.
> Anybody who wants to join has to go through an initiation.
> We cannot waive the rules unless both of the players agree.

Each pronoun in the "either" group takes a singular verb if the noun it refers to is singular and a plural verb if the noun it refers to is plural.

> All of the cake was eaten.
> (*Cake* is singular, so the verb is singular.)

> All of the cupcakes were eaten.
> (*Cupcakes* is plural, so the verb is plural.)

**Assignment:** In Part A of Story 3, there is a box after each indefinite pronoun. Write **S** in the box if the pronoun is singular and **P** if the pronoun is plural. If it is in the "either" group, write **S** if it refers to a singular noun and **P** if it refers to a plural noun. The first one is done for you.

### Story 3: Part A

No one ☒S☒ knows for sure what is the best age to teach children to swim, a panel of three experts agreed last night. They were speaking at a public meeting sponsored by the Clinton YWCA.

One ☐ of the panelists, swimming teacher Mary Sharp, favored early swim lessons much more strongly than the rest of the panel. There were heated exchanges between Sharp and another ☐ of the panelists, pediatrician Dr. Victoria Gordon.

"Anyone ☐ can be taught to swim before he's two years old," said Sharp. "Most ☐ of the children in my classes are under three, and all ☐ of them learn to swim within six months."

In Part B of Story 3, each indefinite pronoun is underlined, and two forms of the verb—singular and plural—are given in parentheses. Circle the form that correctly follows the pronoun. The first one is done for you.

### Story 3: Part B

For Gordon, on the other hand, only part of the question was whether children could be taught to swim at an early age. "<u>All</u> of the publicity about early swim training (has, have) blinded us to the effect it has on the child's development," she said.

Sharp admitted that <u>much</u> (remain, remains) to be learned about the effect of early swim training on child development. "I don't think <u>anything</u> bad (is, are) likely to come of it, though," she said.

The third panelist, psychologist Derek Coutts, expressed the opinion that <u>each</u> of the other panelists (was, were) partly correct. "<u>Some</u> of the truth (is, are) on each side," he said.

In Part C of Story 3, there are errors in the use of verbs after indefinite pronouns. Edit the story to correct these errors. (The marks to use in editing are shown in Instructions for Editing at the beginning of this book.) The first error is corrected for you.

### Story 3: Part C

Coutts said that some of the studies that have been done ~~does~~ <sub>do</sub> suggest that there may be psychological damage from early swim training. He noted, however, that the results of the studies were not clear-cut. "Everybody draws a different conclusion," Coutts said.

In one study group, Coutts noted, most of the children who learned to swim before they were three was later found to have a fear of the water. Another study showed exactly the opposite. "Neither of these conclusions are really firm at this point," Coutts said.

Each of the panelists were given a chance to deliver an opening statement. Then anyone who wanted to ask a question was given the floor. Most of the people who spoke from the floor was happy with their experiences with early swim training for their children.

# 13. Modifiers

Modifiers describe or give extra information about other words. In the following sentences, the modifiers are underlined:

> The <u>tall</u> policeman <u>efficiently</u> directed traffic.
> He performed <u>well</u> under <u>difficult</u> circumstances.
> She would be <u>very</u> <u>happy</u> to see you.

There are two kinds of modifiers, adjectives and adverbs. They describe different things. It is important to know when to use an adjective and when to use an adverb. The trick is to know what you are describing.

## Adjectives

An adjective describes a noun or pronoun. It usually comes just before the word it modifies, but it can also come after a linking verb.

> The <u>old</u> house needed remodeling.
> (*Old* modifies the noun *house.*)
>
> An <u>expensive</u> architect was hired to do the job.
> (*Expensive* modifies the noun *architect.*)
>
> He was <u>angry</u> when they couldn't pay his fee.
> (*Angry* modifies the pronoun *he.*)
>
> The pie tastes <u>delicious</u>.
> (*Delicious* modifies the noun *pie.*)
>
> I felt <u>sad</u> when I heard they were getting a divorce.
> (*Sad* modifies the pronoun *I.*)

## Adverbs

An adverb gives extra information about a verb, an adjective, or another adverb.

> She works <u>carefully</u>.
> (*Carefully* modifies the verb *works.*)
>
> The witness was <u>strangely</u> silent.
> (*Strangely* modifies the adjective *silent.*)
>
> They built the house <u>very quickly</u>.
> (*Quickly* modifies the verb *built*;
> *very* modifies the adverb *quickly.*)

**Adverbs with -ly.** Adverbs can usually be told from adjectives by their spelling. An adverb usually ends in -*ly*. In fact, adverbs are often made by adding -*ly* to adjectives.

> Although he was not a rude person by nature, he behaved rudely the night he was drunk.

Here, *rude* is an adjective modifying *person*, and *rudely* is an adverb modifying *behaved*.

**Adverbs without -ly.** Not all adverbs end in -*ly*. Some examples are *not, here, there, just, indeed, however*, and *nevertheless*.

There are also may adverbs without -*ly* that tell *when* something happens. Some examples are:

| | | | | |
|---|---|---|---|---|
| then | once | always | often | today |
| now | twice | never | sometimes | yesterday |
| | | | seldom | tomorrow |

**Adverbs and adjectives that have the same form.** For some modifiers, the adverb form is the same as the adjective form:

| | | | |
|---|---|---|---|
| early | fast | right | daily |
| late | hard | wrong | weekly |
| high | long | straight | monthly |
| low | ill | | yearly |

> She is a fast runner. She runs fast.

> He gets a weekly paycheck. He is paid weekly.

*Good* **and** *well.* *Good* is an adjective. The corresponding adverb is *well.* As an adverb, *well* describes *how* something is done.

> He is a good player. He plays well.

It is not correct to use *good* as an adverb. Do not write:

> He played good in the game against Courtland.

Instead, write:

> He played well in the game against Courtland.

**Note:** When *well* means *healthy* or *in good health*, it is an adjective.

> I feel well.

**After the verb** *feel.* When you use the verb *feel* to express someone's inner sense of being, it should be followed by an adjective, not an adverb.

> I feel good.

> I feel sorry about what happened.
> I feel bad about what happened.

> I haven't felt healthy all week.
> I haven't felt well all week.

Use an adverb after *feel* only if someone is actually using his hands to do the feeling.

> She felt the rug carefully to make sure all the pins had been picked up.

**Assignment:** In Part A of Story 1, there is a box after certain modifiers. Write **AJ** in the box if the modifier is an adjective. Write **AV** if it is an adverb. The first one is done for you.

### Story 1: Part A

For the last $\boxed{AJ}$ month, Clintonians who turn their TV sets on early $\square$ have been seeing a familiar $\square$ face on their screens.

The face belongs to Rosemary Douglas, who has risen rapidly $\square$ in the competitive $\square$ world of New York journalism. She is now $\square$ an interviewer on the nationally $\square$ broadcast *Morning Journal.*

Ms. Douglas was in Clinton last $\square$ weekend for a quick $\square$ visit. While in town, she dropped into the *Daily* $\square$ *News* office where she once $\square$ worked as a junior $\square$ reporter.

In Part B of Story 1, the underlined modifiers are all adjectives. If the modifier should be an adverb instead, cross out the adjective, and write in the adverb form above it. The first one is done for you.

### Story 1: Part B

"It all happened so ~~quick~~ quickly," she says. "Being a TV reporter has been very exciting."

Ms. Douglas got a job as a researcher with the *Morning Journal* immediate after she arrived in New York on a cold winter day two years ago. She diligent combed through dusty files and made phone calls to collect information for other people's stories.

Then, a month ago, interviewer Carol Strachan sudden quit the show. Unexpected, Ms. Douglas was asked to step into her shoes. Although she admits she was "extreme nervous" the first time she appeared on camera, she handled the situation cool and professional.

In Part C of Story 1, there are errors in the use of modifiers. Sometimes an adverb is used where an adjective would be correct, or an adjective is used where an adverb would be correct. Edit the story to correct these errors. (The marks to use in editing are shown in Instructions for Editing at the beginning of this book.) The first one is done for you.

### Story 1: Part C

Ms. Douglas grew up in Clinton but hasn't ~~real~~ *really* lived here since she went away to college six years ago. "At college, I went to classes fitfully," she says. "I didn't do very good in my courses."

She remembers her summer jobs with the *Daily News* as being "very enjoyable," but when she graduated from college she took off for the brightly lights of New York.

Ms. Douglas exercises regular and enjoys the plays, movies, and concerts that are easy available in New York. "I used to dress very sloppy," she says, "but of course I have to take good care of my appearance now."

# Making Comparisons

Modifiers have special forms that are used for comparing two or more things.

Jenny is <u>older</u> than Rachel, but Rachel is <u>taller</u>.
He was able to walk <u>more</u> <u>easily</u> after his operation than he was before.
Mrs. Simpson is the <u>oldest</u> person in town.
This is the <u>most</u> <u>interesting</u> job I have ever had.

**Degrees of modifiers.** Modifiers change their form to show differences in degree (how much). There are three degrees:

— positive (the basic word)
— comparative (the word used with *more* or the ending *-er*)
— superlative (the word used with *most* or the ending *-est.*)

**Forming comparatives and superlatives.** There are some rules for deciding whether to use the endings *-er* and *-est* or the words *more* and *most* with a modifier. (Never mix the two together. Write *bigger*, not *more bigger*.)

**1**  Short modifiers form the comparative by adding *-er* and the superlative by adding *-est*.

Short modifiers include all those with one syllable and some with two syllables (especially those ending in *-y*).

| Positive | Comparative | Superlative |
|---|---|---|
| small | smaller | smallest |
| fast | faster | fastest |
| big | bigger | biggest |
| late | later | latest |
| easy | easier | easiest |
| early | earlier | earliest |
| narrow | narrower | narrowest |

**2**  Longer modifiers form the comparative by adding the word *more* and the superlative by adding the word *most*.

Longer modifiers include all those with three or more syllables and some with two syllables.

| Positive | Comparative | Superlative |
|---|---|---|
| important | more important | most important |
| respected | more respected | most respected |
| interesting | more interesting | most interesting |
| honest | more honest | most honest |
| famous | more famous | most famous |

**3**  All adverbs with the ending *-ly* use the forms with *more* and *most*.

| Positive | Comparative | Superlative |
|---|---|---|
| quickly | more quickly | most quickly |
| easily | more easily | most easily |
| carefully | more carefully | most carefully |

**4**    Some comparatives and superlatives do not follow the usual pattern:

| Positive | Comparative | Superlative |
|---|---|---|
| bad | worse | worst |
| badly | worse | worst |
| good | better | best |
| well | better | best |
| many | more | most |
| much | more | most |
| little (amount) | less | least |
| far (distance) | farther | farthest |
| far (other uses) | further | furthest |

> This may not be the <u>worst</u> movie I've ever seen, but it's no <u>better</u> than the second <u>worst</u>.
>
> There is <u>little</u> money in the savings account, and even <u>less</u> in the checking account.
>
> Los Angeles is <u>farther</u> from New York than Chicago is.
>
> He went <u>further</u> than he should have in criticizing the mayor.

**5**    The words *less* and *least* can also be added to other modifiers in comparisons.

> Today is warmer than yesterday, but it is <u>less</u> humid.
> Of all her books, this one is the <u>least</u> interesting.

**Using comparatives.** The comparative is used for comparing two things.

> Canada is <u>larger</u> than Mexico.
>
> Who is <u>taller</u>, Roger or William?
>
> Of the two girls, Cheryl usually finishes her homework <u>more</u> quickly than Alice does.

Sometimes the second thing being compared is not mentioned but only understood.

> You will be able to do it <u>faster</u> if you use two hands.
> (*Than you will if you only use one hand* is understood.)

**Using superlatives.** The superlative is used to compare three or more things.

> Which country is the <u>largest</u>—Canada, Mexico, or the United States?
> Of all the employees in the department, he missed work <u>most</u> often.

Sometimes, the other things you are comparing something to are not stated in the sentence.

> Mount Everest is the <u>highest</u> mountain in the world.
> (Mount Everest is being compared to all other mountains in the world.)
>
> This is the <u>most</u> frightening movie I have ever seen.
> (I am comparing this movie to all other movies I have seen.)

**Assignment:** In Part A of Story 2, some modifiers are underlined. These modifiers should be in the comparative or superlative form. Cross out each underlined modifier, and write the correct comparative or superlative form above. The first one is done for you.

### Story 2: Part A

The New York Film Critics awards may be more highly respected, and the
Oscars may be ~~big~~ *bigger*, but last night's Clinton Film Awards may have been the
entertaining of all.

Clinton High School staged the awards dinner to honor 12 students, who
had each made a 10-minute film. The dinner was the school Film Club's
ambitious project to date.

Four awards were given: Good Picture, Imaginative Idea, Skillful Camera
Work, and Good Editing. The Good Picture award went to Bruce Baldwin for
his film *The Clinton Cowboy*. A Hollywood western on a somewhat small
scale, Baldwin's film used local scenery and amateur actors.

In Part B of Story 2, there are errors in the use of comparatives and superlatives. A comparative may be used where a superlative would be correct. A superlative may be used where a comparative would be correct. The wrong form of a comparative or superlative may be used.

Edit the story to correct these errors. (The marks to use in editing are shown in Instructions for Editing at the beginning of this book.) The first one is done for you.

### Story 2: Part B

"This is the ~~happier~~ *happiest* moment of my life," said Baldwin, mimicking the
speeches of Oscar winners. Members of the audience went even farther in
showing their feelings. They tossed dinner rolls at Baldwin, something that
doesn't happen at the more sedate Oscar awards.

Nancy McHugh won the Imaginativest Idea award for her animated film
*Bubble*. Stan Sewell won Most Skillful Camera Work for *Football Game*. Better
Editing went to Kelly Donahue for her documentary study *Weaving*.

Perhaps the most proud person in the room was English teacher Harriet
Fisher, who directed the project. "This is the most enthusiastic group of
students I have ever had," she said. "They did more well than I ever expected."

# 14. Conjunctions

A conjunction is a linking word that connects two or more words or groups of words. Some common conjunctions are *and, or, nor, but, for*, and *yet*.

> The mayor, councilors, <u>and</u> school trustees will all be present at the meeting.
> He scored three touchdowns <u>but</u> was injured in the game.
> You can stay <u>or</u> go; it's all the same to me.

## Two-Part Conjunctions

Some conjunctions consist of more than one word: *both . . . and, either . . . or, neither . . . nor, not only . . . but also*.

> <u>Both</u> Clinton <u>and</u> Courtland are trying to attract new industry.
>
> He is <u>either</u> drunk <u>or</u> crazy; I'm not sure which.
>
> The candidate argued that <u>not only</u> the defense budget <u>but also</u> the space program should be cut.

The different parts of these conjunctions should not be mismatched. Don't write:

> <u>Neither</u> a blizzard <u>or</u> a hurricane will stop her from getting here today.

Instead, write:

> <u>Neither</u> a blizzard <u>nor</u> a hurricane will stop her from getting here today.

**Assignment:** In Part A of Story 1, circle all conjunctions. If the conjunction is made up of two parts, circle both parts. The first one is done for you.

## Story 1: Part A

Clinton will get a new mayor in today's election, (but) there is not likely to be much change in either the town council or the school board.

Voters will choose between Edward Johnson and William Lesage in the race for mayor. Neither Johnson nor Lesage has ever held elective office.

There are six candidates for the five seats on the town council and four candidates for the three school board positions. Not only all five incumbent councilors but also all three sitting school board members are seeking re-election.

In Part B of Story 1, some two-part conjunctions are mismatched. Edit the story to correct these errors. (The marks to use in editing are shown in Instructions for Editing at the beginning of this book.) The first one is done for you.

## Story 1: Part B

Both Johnson ~~or~~ *and* Lesage focused on economic issues during the campaign. Johnson promised to bring more high technology industry to Clinton. He argued that this kind of industry would not only create jobs and make Clinton a better place to live.

Lesage cited what he called "disturbing" statistics showing that Clinton's growth is slower than it was a few years ago. "Either we will go out and actively seek new industry," he said often, "nor we will be left behind."

Neither Johnson or Lesage found fault with outgoing Mayor John Peckford. The two candidates praised Peckford as both a strong leader and an able manager.

# Verbs with Compound Subjects

Sometimes the subject of a sentence consists of two or more nouns (or pronouns) joined by a conjunction. Then it is called a compound subject. The following sentences have compound subjects:

> Joe and Maureen have been married for five years.
> Chicago, Philadelphia, and New Orleans are all bidding for the convention.
> Neither Jack nor Don plays first base as well as I do.

Only a few conjunctions can be used to form compound subjects:

| | | |
|---|---|---|
| and | or | not only . . . but also |
| both . . . and | either . . . or | |
| | neither . . . nor | |

Sometimes compound subjects are followed by singular verbs, and sometimes they are followed by plural verbs. There are different rules depending on which conjunction is used to form the compound subject.

**1**   When a compound subject is joined with *and* or *both . . . and*, use a plural verb.

> Macrame, conversational Spanish, and art appreciation are offered by the continuing education division.

> Both mail delivery and bus service have been running behind schedule.

**2**   When a compound subject is joined with *or, either . . . or, neither . . . nor,* or *not only . . . but also*:

**2-a**   Use a singular verb if the subject closest to the verb is singular.

> The Clinton Pizza Palace or Giuseppe's Pizzeria has Neapolitan-style pizza.

> Either the Mahoneys or Marion Faulkner was living in that house when I first moved here.

**2-b**   Use a plural verb if the subject closest to the verb is plural.

> Neither the West Auburn Raiders nor the Courtland Indians have won as many games as our team.

> Not only mango jam but also fresh mangoes are now available at the One-Stop Supermarket.

**Note:** *As well as* and *along with* do not form compound subjects. They simply introduce extra information. The subject is the word or words that come before *as well as* or *along with*.

> Mayor Johnson along with three town councilors is sponsoring the resolution.

The subject is *Mayor Johnson*, so the verb is singular.

> Italians as well as other Europeans were attracted to America by the prospect of a better life.

The subject is *Italians*, so the verb is plural.

**Assignment:** In Part A of Story 2, circle all compound subjects. The first one is done for you.

### Story 2: Part A

ARIES, Mar. 21 to Apr. 19: (Family and friendship) are featured today. You and your associates are drawn closer together.

TAURUS, Apr. 20 to May 20: An Aquarius as well as a Scorpio plays a prominent role today. Legal affairs and taxes are emphasized.

GEMINI, May 21 to June 20: Your cycle highlights cooperation and partnership. A new business venture or job prospect comes to light.

CANCER, June 21 to July 22: Venus and Mercury influence you today. Their message is favorable if you know how to read it.


In Part B of Story 2, whenever a verb follows a compound subject, two possible forms of the verb—a singular form and a plural form—are given in parentheses. Circle the correct verb form. The first one is done for you.

### Story 2: Part B

LEO, July 23 to Aug. 22: Love and marriage (is, (are)) emphasized. A Taurus or a Virgo (enter, enters) the picture.

VIRGO, Aug. 23 to Sept. 22: The moon and planets (is, are) in a favorable position. Not only happiness but also financial gain (is, are) within your reach today.

LIBRA, Sept. 23 to Oct. 22: Worries or anxiety about your career (weigh, weighs) heavily today. Either an Aries or a Pisces (help, helps) you overcome your fears.

In Part C of Story 2, there are errors in the use of verbs after compound subjects. Edit the story to correct these errors. (The marks to use in editing are shown in Instructions for Editing at the beginning of this book.) The first one is done for you.

### Story 2: Part C

SCORPIO, Oct. 23 to Nov. 21: Both luck and skill ~~is~~ <sup>are</sup> needed today. Either friendship or love is darkened by a cloud.

SAGITTARIUS, Nov. 22 to Dec. 21: A Capricorn along with a Gemini are prominent. Travel and communication is emphasized.

CAPRICORN, Dec. 22 to Jan. 19: Not only your charm but also your abilities helps win you new friends today. Your career situation improves.

AQUARIUS, Jan. 20 to Feb. 18: Mars and Jupiter are in a favorable conjunction. Neither old problems nor new concerns is serious today.

PISCES, Feb. 19 to Mar. 20: A Leo of the same sex or a Sagittarius of the opposite sex have a surprise for you. Don't be caught off guard.

# Subordinating Conjunctions

A subordinating conjunction introduces a dependent clause. When you use a subordinating conjunction, choose the word carefully. Using a different one can often change the meaning of a sentence.

> She was in perfect health <u>until</u> she stopped taking the drug.
> She was in perfect health <u>after</u> she stopped taking the drug.

In the first sentence, the drug made her healthy. In the second sentence, the drug made her sick.

Subordinating conjunctions can be grouped according to their function.

**Group 1** conjunctions introduce clauses that tell *when* the action happens.

| | | | |
|---|---|---|---|
| after | before | until | whenever |
| as | since | when | while |

Most of these houses have been built <u>since</u> the war ended.

This area floods <u>whenever</u> there is heavy rain.

**Group 2** conjunctions introduce clauses that tell *why* the action happens.

| | | | |
|---|---|---|---|
| as | because | since | whereas |

Schools are closed today <u>because</u> buses cannot get through the snow.

<u>Since</u> no one will second your motion, it cannot be discussed.

**Group 3** conjunctions introduce clauses that tell the *purpose* of the action.

| | |
|---|---|
| so that | in order that |

The police blocked the road <u>so that</u> no cars could get through.

Governor Ryan signed the bill <u>in order that</u> swift action could be taken.

**Group 4** conjunctions introduce clauses that tell *under what conditions* the action happens.

| | | | | | |
|---|---|---|---|---|---|
| although | even though | if | provided that | unless | while |

<u>If</u> Emily scores a 9 on the uneven parallel bars, she will win the overall championship.

<u>Unless</u> economic conditions change, the company will show a loss for the year.

**Assignment:** In Part A of Story 3, circle all subordinating conjunctions. The first one is done for you.

### Story 3: Part A

(So that) he could avoid conviction on a rape charge, Richard Pollock pleaded guilty yesterday to a lesser charge of assault.

Judge Lawrence Spivak will hand down sentence tomorrow when he has finished reviewing the evidence against Pollock.

According to police, Pollock pointed a knife at a woman on Main Street before he forced her into his car. He then took her out to Highway 14 and threatened to beat her if she did not submit to him.

In Part B of Story 3, each blank indicates a place where a subordinating conjunction should be. For each blank, choose a subordinating conjunction from the above lists and write it in the blank. Be sure that each sentence and the story as a whole make sense. The subordinating conjunctions in the lists may be used more than once. The first one is done for you.

### Story 3: Part B

The identity of the woman who brought charges against Pollock has not been released _because_ she fears reprisals.

_____ Pollock's lawyer, Murray Smith, said he thought his client would be acquitted on the charge of rape, Pollock agreed to plead guilty to the lesser assault charge. Pollock will receive a 10-year sentence _____ Judge Spivak decides to impose the maximum penalty.

_____ Pollock has not denied that the events reported to the police did take place, he maintained that he was "just kidding" and it was all a joke. Smith was reportedly preparing an insanity defense for his client _____ his chances for acquittal would be maximized.

In Part C of Story 3, some sentences do not make sense because the wrong subordinating conjunctions have been used. Edit the story to correct these errors. (The marks to use in editing are shown in Instructions for Editing at the beginning of this book.) The first one is done for you.

## Story 3: Part C

Pollock was the first person to be charged with rape in Clinton ~~before~~ *since* Jack Norris was convicted on a rape charge four years ago. Local women's groups have expressed concern over the incident although they fear that other similar incidents may follow.

"This could be the start of a cycle of violence against women," said Frances McTeer, president of the Clinton chapter of the Council for Women's Action. Before that happens, McTeer warned, the streets of Clinton could become as unsafe as the streets of large cities.

McTeer said that the law should deal firmly with rapists provided that "women can know that the justice system is protecting them against being attacked on the streets."

# 15. Interjections

Interjections are words that add color and feeling to a sentence. Some common interjections are *Oh, wow, yay, hey, gee, ouch.*

Interjections are often attached to sentences. Then commas are used to set off the interjection from the rest of the sentence.

> <u>Oh</u>, Bill, those are the most beautiful roses I've ever seen.
> <u>Hey</u>, try to be more careful, will you?

Sometimes an interjection stands alone. Then it is usually followed by an exclamation point.

> <u>Well, well</u>! I would never have believed it if I hadn't seen it!

Interjections are used more in speech than in writing. They are seldom used in newswriting, except in direct quotations.

> "<u>Hot dog</u>, we did it!" said a happy Coach Steve Borden in the locker room after the game.

**Assignment:** In the story, circle all interjections. The first one is done for you.

### Story

"Oh, my, I can't believe it," was Michele Crossman's reaction when she found out she had given birth to triplets yesterday. When James Crossman saw his three newborn daughters, he said, "We've got triplets! Holy smoke!"

There were no complications in the birth of the three girls, but it still caused a stir in Clinton Hospital. Nurses with a moment to spare stopped by the nursery to look at the newborns and said, "Ooooh, three of them!"

Even Mrs. Crossman's obstetrician, Dr. Melanie Sampson, was taken aback. "Wow, that's something," she said. "I knew there were two in there, but I didn't know there were three. Gee, I guess medicine still has some surprises."

Perhaps the calmest people in the hospital were the three themselves. Their reaction to their birth was "Waaaaah."

---
# Part 4
# Effective Writing
---

In the last five chapters in this book, we will discuss the principles that good newswriters follow in their writing. These principles will help you in any kind of writing you do. You will learn to:

— write concisely and to the point
— be sure your meaning is clear to the reader
— tell the difference between statements of fact and opinions
— avoid value words when you want to write objectively
— organize your writing so that the important points come first.

# 16. Keep It Short

Newspaper writers follow a number of rules to help make their writing clear and simple. Clarity is important in any form of writing. Learning the rules used by newspaper writers will help make your writing clearer whatever you write. The rules covered in this chapter are:

1. Use short words instead of long words when they mean the same thing.
2. Use short sentences.
3. Use short paragraphs in newswriting.

## Use Short Words

Use short words instead of long words when they mean the same thing.

Bigger words are not necessarily better ones. When a short word and a long word have the same meaning, the short one usually expresses the meaning in a clearer and stronger way. The following sentence has too many long words:

> The perspiration poured down his countenance as he elevated the ponderous weight.

It would be better to write:

> The sweat poured down his face as he lifted the heavy weight.

Similarly,

> Governor Ryan has initiated an investigation into the improper utilization of government automobiles.

would be better written as:

> Governor Ryan has started a probe into the improper use of government cars.

Newspaper writers are trained to use short words whenever possible. Thus, they write *ban* instead of *prohibition, aim* instead of *intention*, and *pact* instead of *covenant*.

Have you ever noticed how much information is given in a newspaper headline? A headline writer has to get across the main idea of a story in a very small space. One way the writer does this is by using short words. Two examples follow.

| | |
|---|---|
| (Too long) | Union requests salary increase |
| (Shorten to) | Union seeks pay hike |
| (Too long) | Senate ratifies weapons agreement |
| (Shorten to) | Senate okays arms pact |

Sometimes, a long word gives more information than a short word. When it does, good writers will often use the long word. Thus,

| | |
|---|---|
| (Vague) | He is proud of his prize flowers. |
| (Clearer) | He is proud of his prize geraniums. |
| (Vague) | She is the author of three books. |
| (Clearer) | She is the author of three biographies. |

But when a long word and a short word give the same information, it is better to use the short one.

**Assignment:** In Part A of Story 1, the underlined words are too long. Cross them out, and replace them with shorter words that mean the same thing. (The marks to use in editing are shown in Instructions for Editing at the beginning of this book.) The first one is done for you.

### Story 1: Part A

A fisherman who ~~aspired~~ *hoped* to catch some trout in the Black River near

Clinton last weekend landed a <u>ferocious</u> South American piranha instead.

Charles Elgie of North Street in Clinton was not <u>cognizant</u> that the

<u>voracious</u> fish was a piranha until Susan Williams, a biologist with the State

Conservation Authority, identified it.

Williams said piranha, which are <u>commonplace</u> in aquariums, are

sometimes released into lakes or rivers when they grow <u>excessively</u> large.

In Part B of Story 1, replace long, difficult words with shorter, easier words that mean the same thing. Change only words, not phrases. (The marks to use in editing are shown in Instructions for Editing at the beginning of this book.) The first one is done for you.

### Story 1: Part B

The piranha, which is ~~indigenous~~ *native* to Brazil, is renowned for its propensity

to attack any animal, including man.

According to Williams, however, Clinton inhabitants who swim in the

Black River should not be apprehensive about being devoured by a piranha.

"There are really very few of them," she affirmed. "They are used to living

in the tropics and can't survive very long in our climate."

In Story 2, find words that are too long, and replace them with shorter words that mean the same thing. (The marks to use in editing are shown in Instructions for Editing at the beginning of this book.)

## Story 2

The state coordinator of the Interfaith Relief Network, Harriet Macaulay, last night expressed her gratitude to Clintonians for the assistance they have provided to victims of famine and pestilence in impoverished countries.

Speaking to a considerable gathering in the Social Hall of All Saints Church, Macaulay declared that Clintonians have been "among the most generous people in the state."

She informed the audience that the money contributed by Clintonians is being utilized to provide sustenance and pharmaceuticals to hungry and sick children.

The Interfaith Relief Network is endeavoring to raise additional money to reinforce its programs in Africa and Asia.

# Use Short Sentences

A short sentence has less room for error than a long one. The writer has fewer words to manage in a short sentence, and the reader can understand the sentence more easily.

There are two ways to correct a sentence that is too long.

**1**    A long sentence can be broken into two shorter ones.

The following sentence contains too much information:

> A Clinton man, Lloyd Randall, 27, of Branch Street, was arrested in Springfield Saturday night and is free on bail while he is being investigated in connection with a rape alleged to have taken place earlier that same evening, according to police.

It would be better if it were broken into two sentences:

> A Clinton man is being investigated in connection with a rape alleged to have taken place Saturday evening, according to police.

> Lloyd Randall, 27, of Branch Street, was arrested in Springfield later that night and is free on bail.

**2**    A long sentence can be rewritten to make it more concise.

The following sentence is too wordy:

> The arrest of Randall came as a consequence of a complaint submitted to police by a woman who is 22 years old and lives in Springfield.

It would be better if it were rewritten as follows:

> A complaint submitted to police by a 22-year-old Springfield woman led to Randall's arrest.

Newswriters try to make their writing more readable and concise by replacing wordy expressions with short, punchy ones. Here are some examples:

| Instead of: | Use: |
| --- | --- |
| 4 o'clock in the afternoon | 4 p.m. |
| in spite of the fact | although |
| true facts | facts (If they're false, they're not facts.) |

Sometimes one longer sentence reads more smoothly than two short ones. Also, writing that contains nothing but short sentences tends to be monotonous. The most effective writing is made up mostly of short sentences with some long ones for variety. Varied sentence length helps make this story about a young swimmer easy to read:

> Jennifer Drury wants to swim in the Olympics.
> And if the seventh-grade student at Clinton Junior High School keeps swimming the way she did in the county championships in Lafayette last weekend, she just might make it.
> Drury dominated the championships by winning four events (two of them in county record time). She finished second in three others and helped the Clinton team win the 400-meter relay by more than eight seconds.
> Her coach, Helen Reynolds, says Drury has "the potential to make our national team in a few years."

**Assignment:** In Part A of Story 3, all the sentences are too long. Shorten each sentence either by breaking it into two sentences or by making it more concise. (The marks to use in editing are shown in Instructions for Editing at the beginning of this book.) The first two sentences are done for you.

## Story 3: Part A

Windows were smashed in three buildings on North Street last night at about 4 ~~o'clock in the morning,~~ *a.m.* causing an estimated $1,000 damage. *This is* ~~in~~ the latest in a series of vandalism incidents that have plagued the north end for about the last three months, according to police.

A woman ~~whose residence is~~ *living* in the north end ~~communicated by telephone~~ *called* ~~with~~ police to ~~provide~~ *tell* them ~~with the information~~ that loud noises could be heard in the neighborhood. ~~but~~ the ~~persons who committed the act of vandalism~~ *vandals* had ~~departed from~~ *left* the scene by the time the police arrived, *however.*

The three stores that were vandalized—Sid's Variety, Modern HairStyling, and Clinton TV Repair—were all closed for the night when the incident happened, and there were no witnesses as most people in the area were asleep.

In spite of the fact that the vandals appear to have made their way into Sid's Variety subsequent to having smashed the window, there was no evidence that any valuable belongings had been taken, police said.

In Part B of Story 3, some sentences are too long, and some are not. Shorten the sentences you think are too long. Either break them into two sentences or make them more concise. (The marks to use in editing are shown in Instructions for Editing at the beginning of this book.)

## Story 3: Part B

Last night's incident was the sixth case of vandalism in the north end since the middle of April, as places of business, private residences, and cars have all been struck by vandals in the three-month period. No other areas of town have been affected.

Police have not arrested any suspects in connection with the incidents.

An investigation is being carried out in the hope of determining who is responsible for the incidents, but police are finding it difficult to make any progress as the vandals are committing these crimes in the nighttime and early morning hours when people in the north end are asleep and there are not many witnesses.

In Story 4, some sentences are too long, and some are not. Shorten the sentences you think are too long. Either break them into two sentences or make them more concise. (The marks to use in editing are shown in Instructions for Editing at the beginning of this book.)

## Story 4

At tonight's meeting of the Clinton Historical Society, the guest speaker, Harvey MacMillan, a teacher at Clinton High School and amateur genealogist, will describe how there are people in Clinton who are descended from such notable historical figures as Julius Caesar, King Henry VIII of England, and George Washington.

Prior to Mr. MacMillan's address, the meeting will engage in a discussion of the effort being undertaken by the Historical Society at the present time to obtain financial support for the restoration of the old Wilson house on South Main Street, which has fallen into a state of disrepair.

The meeting will begin at 7 o'clock in the evening in the Arthur Walsh Memorial Room of the Clinton Public Library.

# Use Short Paragraphs in Newswriting

Paragraphs are much shorter in newswriting than in any other form of writing. A news paragraph is usually made up of only one or two sentences. Newswriters try to write paragraphs that are no longer than four typewritten lines.

Short paragraphs are important in newswriting because news columns are narrow, and long paragraphs would be hard to read. Using short paragraphs also allows the reader to absorb information in small bits.

Here is an example of a news story in short paragraphs.

> Clinton Town Council has decided to submit the school budget issue to a referendum.
>
> Clinton residents will be asked to vote May 29 on the controversial budget. A petition signed by more than 300 property owners asked for the referendum. Signers of the petition felt that projected spending for expansion of the elementary school was too high.
>
> "This is the kind of issue that only the voters can decide," said Mayor Edward Johnson after last night's council meeting. He added that he hoped voters would decide to approve the budget.

In other forms of writing, deciding when to begin a new paragraph is a matter of judgment, not rules. Paragraphs usually consist of several sentences. But it is best not to make your paragraphs too long. In any form of writing, a paragraph should express a single idea. When you begin writing about a new idea, you should start a new paragraph.

**Assignment:** Divide Story 5 into paragraphs as a news story. Put the paragraph symbol, ⁊ , at the beginning of each sentence that should start a new paragraph. The first one is done for you.

### Story 5

North county farmer Alex Lowe sings every day for an appreciative audience—his dairy herd of 52 cows. ⁊ The live concert helps the cows produce more milk, Lowe believes. "I can't quote you figures, but I know they've been more productive since I started singing to them," he says. Before he started singing, Lowe used to play recorded music for the cows. He says that helped too, but "somehow the cows like hearing me sing better." Lowe's concerts in the barn include Broadway tunes, opera, and "sometimes a song or two that I make up myself, just for the cows." In addition to being a farmer, Lowe is also an avid amateur musician. He has organized a string quartet that gets together to play chamber music every Thursday night in Clinton.

# 17. Make It Clear

We have discussed using short words, short sentences, and short paragraphs to make your writing clear and simple. In this chapter, we will learn three more rules that lead to clear writing:

1. Make sure your words are in the right place.
2. Use the same form for all the words in a list.
3. Use the active rather than the passive voice.

## Make Sure Your Words Are in the Right Place

Words in a sentence often refer to other words. These words should be as close to each other as possible. Otherwise, the meaning of the sentence may not be clear. You, the writer, know what you want to say. To make sure that your meaning is clear to the reader as well, you have to read your work very carefully.

The following example is not clear to the reader.

> Although they are known to be dangerous, crops are still being sprayed with the insecticides.

Does *they* refer to *crops* or *insecticides*? In other words, is it the crops or the insecticides that are dangerous? The sentence would be clearer if it were written:

> Although the insecticides are known to be dangerous, they are still being used to spray crops.

Here is another confusing sentence:

> A professor of history in England, King Arthur has been Dr. McClung's main interest for the last 20 years.

Who is the professor of history, King Arthur or Dr. McClung? If the sentence were written as below there would be no confusion.

> Dr. McClung, a professor of history in England, has been mainly interested in King Arthur for the last 20 years.

Here is another example:

> At this time of year, motorists see fields of daffodils driving into Clinton.

Does *driving into Clinton* refer to *the motorists* or *the fields of daffodils*? Of course, it is the motorists who drive into Clinton, not the fields of daffodils. To make it clearer, the sentence should be rewritten:

> At this time of year, motorists driving into Clinton see fields of daffodils.

**Assignment:** In Part A of Story 1, the writer has not made sure that all the words are in the right place. Each underlined word or group of words refers to another word in the same sentence. Find the word the underlined words refer to, and circle it. The first one is done for you.

### Story 1: Part A

Shoppers turned their heads yesterday when they saw a (car) in Valley View Mall about as long as a trailer truck.

Looking through the window, what was inside the car came as even more of a surprise to the curious shoppers. Between the front seat and the back seat, the car sports a small swimming pool, which also has three telephones, a color television set, and a bar.

Built in California, the owner of the car, Michael Peterson of Beverly Hills, is taking it on a cross-country tour.

Describing himself as a "professional stockbroker and amateur inventor," the car took Peterson four years to build and cost more than $1 million.

In Part B of Story 1, some of the sentences are confusing because the writer has put words in the wrong place. Make these sentences clearer by changing the order of the words. (The marks to use in editing are shown in Instructions for Editing at the beginning of this book.) The first one is done for you.

### Story 1: Part B

*The idea first came to Peterson,*
∧ A swimming enthusiast who has three pools in his Beverly Hills backyard, ~~the idea first came to Peterson~~ when he thought of "how much time I was wasting on California freeways."

The car is a "full-size working model," Peterson says. He plans to produce a limited number of "pool cars" in a factory in Los Angeles, which he will sell to buyers willing to pay the asking price of $2 million.

So far, one person has expressed interest in buying a "pool car," who wants to use it for publicity, Peterson says.

Peterson and the car spent three hours in Clinton before going on to Courtland, where they planned to spend the night.

In Story 2, some of the sentences are confusing because the writer has put words in the wrong places. Make these sentences clearer by changing the order of the words. (The marks to use in editing are shown in Instructions for Editing at the beginning of this book.)

## Story 2

A Springfield man has leased the first floor of the Atkins Building on Main Street, who plans to produce computer software there.

A 27-year-old graduate of Springfield State College, the new business is the brainchild of Felix Kramer, who hopes to produce software for the school and home computer markets.

The deal was announced yesterday in a press conference at Town Hall, involving a three-year lease at $100,000 per year.

Kramer described the Main Street site as an "ideal location" for his expanding business at the press conference, which he now operates in a small storefront in downtown Springfield.

Representing the Town of Clinton, Economic Development Director Joanne Burgess said she was pleased that "a modern industry with potential for growth is coming to town."

# Use the Same Form for All Words in a List

Words that have the same form are called parallel. Nouns, verbs, and modifiers can all be made parallel.

> (Nouns)
> cows, sheep, and goats
>
> (Verbs: *-ing* forms)
> running, jumping, and playing
>
> (Verbs: infinitive forms)
> to camp, to swim, to sail, and to hike
>
> (Adjectives)
> warm, windy, and rainy
>
> (Adverbs)
> quickly, cheerfully, and well
>
> (Comparative degree of adjectives)
> bigger, faster, more powerful, but less expensive

In the last example, the modifiers are parallel because they are all comparatives, even though the first two use the *-er* form, the third one uses *more*, and the last one uses *less*.

A list of superlatives would also be parallel, even if it included words with *-est*, with *most* and with *least*. A list that mixed comparatives and superlatives would not be parallel, however.

Note that nouns do not have to be all singular or all plural to be parallel.

> money, credit cards, and a driver's license

**Use parallel word forms.** When two or more words are grouped in a list, they must be parallel in form. Places to watch for are compound subjects, compound verbs, or compound objects. (A compound object is a group of nouns that follows a verb or preposition.)

> <u>Cows</u>, <u>sheep</u>, and <u>goats</u> are raised on the 100-acre farm.
>
> She sets aside time in the morning <u>for running</u> and in the afternoon <u>for playing</u> tennis.
>
> In her job, she is expected <u>to take</u> dictation, <u>to type</u> 20 letters a day, and <u>to answer</u> the telephone.
>
> People come here in the summer <u>to camp</u>, <u>to swim</u>, <u>to sail</u>, and <u>to hike</u>.
>
> The weather here in April is <u>warm</u>, <u>windy</u>, and <u>rainy</u>.

When the words in a list are next to one another, it is usually fairly easy to spot mistakes with non-parallel words.

> People come here in the summer for <u>camping</u>, <u>swimming</u>, <u>sailing</u>, and <u>to hike</u>.
>
> The weather here in April is <u>warm</u>, <u>windy</u>, and <u>some rain</u>.

When the words in a list or parts of a compound sentence are farther apart, it is not always easy to spot mistakes.

> She sets aside time in the morning <u>for running</u> and in the afternoon <u>to play</u> tennis.
>
> In her job, she is expected <u>to take</u> dictation, <u>to type</u> 20 letters a day, and <u>answers</u> the telephone.

**How to correct mistakes.** Because a sentence with non-parallel words mixes two word forms, often there are two ways to correct it. Decide which word form you want to use, and use it consistently.

For example, look at this incorrect sentence:

> Children in the nursery school learn singing and to paint.

It can be written correctly in two ways:

> Children in the nursery school learn to sing and to paint.
> Children in the nursery school learn singing and painting.

**Assignment:** In Part A of Story 3, underline all of the parallel words that you find in any sentence. Not all sentences have parallel words, however. The first sentence that does is completed for you.

### Story 3: Part A

Clinton-born boxer Kid Raney returns to the ring tonight for the first time in six months. Raney has <u>won</u> six and <u>lost</u> only one of his nine professional bouts.

Raney will fight Bill Dalton of Chicago in a 10-round bout. A win could be a major boost to Raney's career and possibly put him in line for a shot at the world lightweight championship.

The 24-year-old Raney is reported to be fully recovered from injuries to his neck, shoulders, and chest suffered in his last bout.

Dalton's speed, strength, and agility will make him a strong opponent for Raney. The veteran Chicago fighter has a 22-5-3 record and a proven ability to outlast inexperienced opponents.

In Part B of Story 3, there are groups of words that are not parallel. The words in each group are underlined. Edit the story so that each group of words is parallel in form. You may need to change other words besides the underlined ones. (The marks to use in editing are shown in Instructions for Editing at the beginning of this book.) The first group is done for you.

### Story 3: Part B

Dalton's career has been marred recently by legal problems, however, including an <u>arrest</u> for narcotics possession and ~~convicted twice~~ _two convictions_ ∧ for drunken driving.

Raney's last fight was declared a draw in the sixth round when both fighters were <u>injured</u>, <u>bleeding</u>, and <u>couldn't</u> continue.

Raney was an outstanding high school <u>boxer</u>, a Golden Gloves <u>champion</u>, and <u>won</u> an Olympic bronze medal before turning pro.

In Story 4, there may be lists and compound verbs, subjects, and objects in which the words are not parallel. Edit the story so that all such groups of words are in parallel form. (The marks to use in editing are shown in Instructions for Editing at the beginning of this book.)

### Story 4

Clintonians will be amused at the antics of the clowns, amazed at the feats of the acrobats, and thrill at the sight of the wild animals as the circus comes to town for its annual visit.

The Burke Brothers Circus is setting up its tent in Brownlee Field for a matinee and evening performance tomorrow and in the evening again on Friday.

New with the circus this year is high-wire artist Pepe Rodriguez, who has been a circus star in Mexico, Brazil, and performed in Spain.

Tickets are $4 for adults and $2 for children.

# Use the Active Rather Than the Passive Voice

When people read a news story, they want to find out what happened. They want to know what the action is. Verbs are the action part of a sentence. To emphasize action, newswriters usually put their verbs in the active voice.

**Active voice.** A verb in the active voice directly follows the doer of the action—the subject. It tells what the subject did, is doing, or will do. In the following sentences, the underlined verbs are in the active voice:

> The Clinton Tigers defeated the Courtland Indians 23-17 yesterday.
>
> Mayor Edward Johnson is studying a proposal to develop High Street between Water and Branch streets.
>
> Book critic Elizabeth Neary will address tonight's meeting of the Clinton Literary Society on "New Trends in the American Novel."

Other examples of verbs in the active voice are:

> The council has decided      I think
> The Tigers were losing       She administers

**Passive voice.** In the passive voice, the doer comes *after* the verb with a *by* phrase. Sometimes the sentence may not tell you who the doer is at all. The verb itself changes: the correct form of *be* is placed before the main part of the verb. In the following sentences, the underlined verbs are in the passive voice:

> The Courtland Indians were defeated 23-17 by the Clinton Tigers yesterday.
>
> A proposal for the redevelopment of High Street between Water and Branch streets is being studied.
>
> Tonight's meeting of the Clinton Literary Society will be addressed by book critic Elizabeth Neary on "New Trends in the American Novel."

Other examples of verbs in the passive voice are:

> The letter has been delivered      I am seen
> He was injured                     We are being taxed

**Why use the active voice?** The active voice gets your message across more directly and clearly than the passive voice. Using the active voice also makes for a more concise sentence.

Sometimes the writer doesn't know who the doer of the action is. Sometimes the writer wants to emphasize the person or thing the action was done to. In these cases, the passive voice may be used.

> A convenience store on Billings Street was robbed yesterday and $193.48 in cash was taken from the cash register. Police have not identified any suspects in the robbery.
>
> Edward Johnson was re-elected yesterday to a third term as mayor of Clinton.

Even when you don't know who the doer is, however, there is often a way around the passive voice. You can use a general term as the subject and change the verb to an active one.

> Robbers yesterday broke into a convenience store on Billings Street and took $193.48 in cash from the cash register. Police have not identified any suspects in the robbery.

> Clinton voters yesterday re-elected Edward Johnson to a third term as mayor of Clinton.

You can also choose a different verb in the active voice.

> Edward Johnson yesterday won a third term as mayor of Clinton.

Whenever possible, especially in newswriting, the writer should identify the doer of the action and put the verb in the active voice.

**Assignment:** In Part A of Story 5, some of the underlined verbs are in the active voice, and some are in the passive voice. If a verb is active, write **A** in the box after the verb. If a verb is passive, write **P** in the box. The first one is done for you.

### Story 5: Part A

The Davis Molding Company, one of Clinton's largest employers, is being threatened ☐P☐ with a strike.

Local 178 of the Plastic and Chemical Workers of America, which represents ☐ 125 Davis employees, is seeking ☐ a $3-an-hour wage increase over two years. A $1.75-an-hour increase has been offered ☐ by the company.

Local 178 president Dan O'Neil said ☐ yesterday that the strike will begin ☐ next Friday unless an agreement is reached ☐ with the company.

In Part B of Story 5, verbs that are in the passive voice are underlined. Rewrite the sentences containing these verbs so that they are in the active voice. (The marks to use in editing are shown in Instructions for Editing at the beginning of this book.) The first one is done for you.

**Story 5: Part B**

*Union and company negotiators resolved*

$\wedge$ Several other issues—job security, working conditions, and vacations— ~~were resolved~~ last week~~, by union and company negotiators~~. No agreement could be reached on the question of wages, however.

According to O'Neil, negotiations have not been carried out in good faith by the company. Poor sales and declining markets were the reasons that were cited by Davis Molding managing director Mark Mackenzie for the company's failure to meet the union's demands.

The Davis plant was shut down by a strike four years ago over the issue of union recognition. At that time, the Davis employees had just been signed up by the Plastic and Chemical Workers.

In Part C of Story 5, some verbs are in the passive voice. Find these verbs, and rewrite the sentences containing them so that they are in the active voice.

**Story 5: Part C**

The company was purchased 18 months ago by Diversified Investments Corp. of Newark, N.J., from its original owner, Hugh Davis of Clinton. O'Neil says management's position has hardened since then.

"At least Hugh Davis had a sense of the company's responsibility to this town," O'Neil said yesterday. The union leader maintains that, since the purchase, only profit and loss figures have been considered by the company. Its social responsibility has been neglected, he says.

Mackenzie, however, argues that economic facts have to be taken into account by the union. "We're competing with plants in South Korea and Taiwan," he says. "We can't price ourselves out of the market."

Negotiations will be resumed by union and company representatives Monday morning.

# 18. State Facts, Not Opinions

In this chapter, you will learn to distinguish between fact and opinion in different forms of writing. You will also practice writing objective news stories in which only facts are presented.

## Facts and Opinions

In all forms of writing, it is important to distinguish between facts (things we know are true) and opinions or feelings (things we think, believe, hope, or wish are true).

This distinction is very important in newswriting. The reader of a news story expects to read facts, not the writer's opinions. Thus, in writing a news story, you must avoid statements of opinion. A news story that contains only facts and not the writer's opinions is called an objective story.

Most other forms of writing—even in newspapers—allow the writer to express both facts and opinions. In an editorial, the newspaper expresses its opinion about some item in the news. In a movie review, the reviewer says what he or she thinks of the movie being discussed. A gardening columnist might express his or her opinion of a particular seed or mulch.

Skillful editorial writers, reviewers, or columnists will make sure that their opinions are backed up by facts, however.

When you read, you should be able to tell what is a fact and what is the writer's opinion. That way, you can make up your own mind about the subject the writer is discussing.

(Fact)      Linda has brown hair.

(Opinion)    Linda has beautiful hair.

A statement identifying the color of a person's hair is objective. It simply reports something you see. A statement that a person's hair is "beautiful" is a value judgment. What some people find beautiful, others may not.

(Fact)      Thomas Jefferson was the third president of the United States.

(Opinion)    Thomas Jefferson was the greatest president the United States ever had.

Anyone who looks up the list of the U.S. presidents will find that Thomas Jefferson was the third. On the other hand, while some people might think that Jefferson was the greatest president, other people might think that some other president was greater.

(Fact)     The new generating station has a capacity of 5,000 kilowatts.

(Opinion)  The new generating station will solve Clinton's electricity problems.

Engineers can measure the capacity of a generating station. Whether or not the station will "solve Clinton's electricity problems" is not so certain. Perhaps people will use more electricity than the experts think, and Clinton will still have problems, even with the new station.

**Assignment:** Stories 1 and 2 contain facts and opinions. There is a box after each statement. Write an **F** in the box if the statement is a fact. Write an **O** if the statement is an opinion. The first one is done for you.

### Story 1

The Clinton Choral Society presented its annual concert last night. ☐F

Unfortunately, the performance was not as good as last year's. ☐

The first part of the concert was a medley of Broadway tunes from *My Fair Lady, Hello Dolly!, A Little Night Music, A Chorus Line*, and *Evita*. ☐ Many of these numbers were well done, ☐ but Maryann Hays, the Choral Society's star soloist for the last three years, was not in top form. ☐ She did not receive the standing ovations that greeted her last year. ☐

The Broadway medley was followed by a group of songs by the 19th-century composer Stephen Foster. ☐ These featured tenor Conrad Ross, a new member of the society. ☐ Ross showed promise, ☐ although he sometimes overplayed the sentimental aspect of Foster's songs. ☐

The evening closed with a selection of hymns, ☐ which are usually the Choral Society's strength. ☐ The inspirational quality that the society's hymn-singing usually has ☐ was missing last night, however. ☐

The audience of 500 appeared to enjoy last night's concert, ☐ despite its faults. ☐ Clinton can be proud of its Choral Society, even on an off night. ☐

## Story 2

People in Clinton who like Italian food generally make it at home. ☐ This is because it is very hard to find a restaurant in the area that serves good Italian food. ☐ A new restaurant has opened on Route 27 ☐ that should change that situation, however. ☐

Mama Teresa's is located about three miles north of Clinton in a converted farmhouse. ☐ Inside, the restaurant looks like a country kitchen. ☐ The owner-chef is Teresa Impellitteri, who came here from Italy only five years ago. ☐

Mama Teresa's specializes in pasta dishes. ☐ Mrs. Impellitteri makes her own pasta, ☐ and it is tender but firm and very tasty. ☐ I had *spaghetti alla carbonara*, which is spaghetti in a sauce made of cheese, eggs, onions, and bacon. ☐ The dish was attractively garnished with herbs ☐ and was very satisfying. ☐ My companion's linguini with clam sauce, made with fresh clams, ☐ was equally good. ☐

We also had an antipasto, ☐ which contained several unusual stuffed and marinated vegetables. ☐ It was far above any other antipasto in the area. ☐ Our dessert, a selection of Italian pastries, was quite ordinary, however. ☐ Mama Teresa's also serves a variety of European coffees. ☐ My espresso was excellent. ☐

The bill for two came to $19.25, ☐ not unreasonable for a meal of this quality. ☐ No credit cards are accepted. ☐ Mama Teresa's is open Tuesday through Sunday from noon to 9 p.m. ☐ It is closed Mondays. ☐

# Loaded Words

Opinions are not always expressed through direct statements. Sometimes, we make our opinions known by the words we use to describe something. Some words and phrases create a positive association, some create a negative association, and some are neutral.

**Example 1:**    (Positive)
As mayor, he has shown flexibility and an ability to learn.

(Negative)
As mayor, he has betrayed everything he ever stood for.

(Neutral)
As mayor, he has made decisions that were different from positions he took before he held the office.

**Example 2:**    (Positive)
She has worked tirelessly to preserve her neighborhood.

(Negative)
She has been a stubborn opponent of progress in her neighborhood.

(Neutral)
For three years, she has led a committee to stop the construction of a new shopping mall in her neighborhood.

In writing news stories, you should avoid expressing your opinion directly. You should also express things in as neutral a manner as possible. Avoid words or phrases that influence the reader one way or the other. A sentence such as the following has no place in a news story:

> As the result of a generous contribution of $25,000 by Hugh Davis, Clinton Hospital will purchase new CAT scan equipment and be on the frontiers of modern medicine.

It should be edited so that it reads as follows:

> As the result of a $25,000 contribution by Hugh Davis, Clinton Hospital will purchase new CAT scan equipment.

In the same way,

> The irresponsible, power-crazed Plastic and Chemical Workers have threatened to call a strike at the Davis Molding Company, jeopardizing the future of industry in Clinton.

should be edited to read:

> The Plastic and Chemical Workers have said they may call a strike at the Davis Molding Company.

**Assignment:** Some statements in Story 3 are positive, some are negative, and some are neutral. In the box after each statement, write + if the statement is positive, - if it is negative, and **N** if it is neutral. The first one is done for you.

## Story 3

For the last four months, Clintonians have had to put up with pale winter tomatoes, iceberg lettuce that feels like cardboard, and tasteless frozen vegetables. ☐(−)

Now, however, they can again enjoy the natural goodness and nutritional value of fresh vegetables ☐ as Garden-Fresh Fruit and Vegetable Mart reopens for the spring and summer season. ☐

As usual, Garden-Fresh will offer both fresh-picked produce from local farms and outstanding fruits and vegetables from all over the country and abroad. ☐ Right now, Garden-Fresh is featuring crisp California greens, succulent Idaho potatoes, and juicy Florida oranges. ☐

Garden-Fresh Fruit and Vegetable Mart is open Monday through Saturday from 9 a.m. to 6 p.m. and Sunday from noon to 5 p.m. ☐

Story 4 is written to make the reader think positively about a new store. Edit the story to make it an objective report about the store's opening. Use only neutral statements. Take out any statements that are designed to influence the reader's thinking. (The marks to use in editing are shown in Instructions for Editing at the beginning of this book.)

## Story 4

Clinton will join the modern world next week when a new Computer Age store opens on Main Street.

Computer Age will have everything for the new computer generation. Not only will it carry a full line of computers, but it will also have the absolute latest in software and accessories.

As part of its grand opening, Computer Age is making an incredible offer: a free video game with any purchase of $50 or more. Customers can take advantage of this once-in-a-lifetime offer any time until September 23.

Computer Age will be located at the site of the former Grant's Variety, across Main Street from Jackson's Pharmacy.

# Attributing Opinions

Although newswriters are supposed to keep their own opinions out of news stories, they often report the opinions of others. Newspapers often report what politicians, officials, ministers, scientists, business leaders, or ordinary people have said in speeches, statements, or interviews.

What somebody said may be only that person's opinion. That the person said it, however, is a fact.

**Example 1:** (Opinion)
Clinton Hospital is the most backward institution in the state.

(Fact)
"Clinton Hospital is the most backward institution in the state," says Dr. Joseph Aylward, who has been denied permission to practice at the hospital.

**Example 2:** (Opinion)
Clinton is the best place in the entire country to invest your money.

(Fact)
"Clinton is the best place in the entire country to invest your money," said Mayor Edward Johnson yesterday, speaking to a group of visiting Japanese businessmen.

**Example 3:** (Opinion)
A new bridge over the railroad tracks is vital to the future of Clinton.

(Fact)
West-end residents argued at last night's town council meeting that a new bridge over the railroad tracks is vital to the future of Clinton.

When newswriters report somebody's opinion, they must make it clear *whose* opinion it is. This is called attributing the opinion. Thus, in the last example sentence, the opinion that a new bridge is vital to the future of Clinton is attributed to west-end residents.

**Direct quotations.** A newswriter can attribute an opinion in one of two ways. In the sentences about Clinton Hospital and the investment climate in Clinton, the speakers' exact words have been used, and their statements have been enclosed in quotation marks. This is called direct quotation.

**Indirect quotations.** In the sentence about the bridge, the west-end residents' exact words have not been used, but the main point of their argument has been reported. This is called indirect quotation. No quotation marks are used in indirect quotations.

The word *that* is often used to introduce an indirect quotation:

> The arresting officer, Ian Holt, reported that the car went through the red light at forty miles an hour.

Sometimes the indirect quotation follows directly after *said* (or whatever verb is used to indicate attribution):

> Coach Steve Borden said his team is in top physical shape for tomorrow's game against Elmira.

> Borden called pitcher Chuck Lang the backbone of the Clinton team.

A phrase beginning with *according to* also often indicates an indirect quotation:

> According to Clinton pediatrician Dr. James V. Lyon, flu may be a serious problem this winter.

In newswriting, the attribution often comes after the indirect quotation:

> The state is likely to increase its local aid budget next year, Representative Elliott Woodsworth said yesterday.

Note that quotation marks can be used only if the speaker's words are reported exactly as he said them. In the last sentence, we do not know that *the state is likely to increase its local aid budget next year* was exactly what Woodsworth said. We know only that this is the substance of what he said. If Woodsworth did use those exact words, the sentence could be written:

> "The state is likely to increase its local aid budget next year," Representative Elliott Woodsworth said yesterday.

Reporters try to vary the way they attribute opinions in news stories. A story with no direct quotations can look dull, but too many quotation marks can be distracting. A skillful newswriter uses a mixture of direct and indirect quotations.

**Assignment:** Story 5 contains both direct and indirect quotations. Underline each direct quotation once and underline each indirect quotation twice. The first paragraph is done for you.

### Story 5

Speaking to the Rotary Club yesterday, Police Chief Ted Mulvaney called Clinton "one of the most law-abiding towns of its size in the state." He said that the town owes its low crime rate to a well-equipped, professional police force.

According to Mulvaney, the new communications equipment purchased by the force three years ago has greatly improved its ability to prevent crime.

"But the most important factor in the high standards of our police force," Mulvaney said, "is the quality of the men and women who work on it. I know all of Clinton is proud of them."

The police chief said crime detection and prevention is much more scientific than it used to be, and today's police officer has to be a highly-trained professional. The use of computers in police work is an important new development, he added.

"We shouldn't forget the human element, though," Mulvaney said. "A police officer may have a degree in criminology and be a whiz with computers, but if he can't make a woman whose pocketbook has been snatched feel that he's there to help her, I don't want him on my force."

Story 6 contains both attributed and unattributed opinions. In the box after each statement of opinion, write **A** if the opinion is attributed, and **U** if it is unattributed. The first one is done for you.

### Story 6

If something isn't done soon, Clinton High School will turn into a drug-ridden den of iniquity. [U]

At a special meeting last night, Clinton parents expressed anger and concern about drug use in the high school. ☐ "We just don't understand how this could have been allowed to happen," said Joanne McGibbon of Pleasant Street. ☐

The School Committee is doing the best it can to deal with the problem. ☐ "This is a national problem, and it won't be solved overnight," said School Committee member Deborah Schreyer. ☐

The School Committee's best efforts are not good enough, however. ☐ Anthony Marler of Landon Street said that the school could have done more to combat drug use through drug education and security. ☐ "My daughter tells me that marijuana is being sold right in the school cafeteria," he said. ☐ "That's the school's responsibility." ☐

Other parents blamed the influx of students from nearby Washburne for the drug problem. ☐ Since the Washburne students started coming to Clinton High School, there has been a rowdy element in the school. ☐

Story 7 is a report of a speech by Fred Fleming, coach of the Clinton High School basketball team. All of the opinions expressed in the story are Fleming's, but the writer has neglected to attribute some of the opinions to him. Edit the story so that all the opinions are attributed to Fleming.

### Story 7

Sports are an important part of a boy's or girl's education, according to Clinton High School basketball coach Fred Fleming.

"Sports help build character as well as physical strength," Fleming told the annual fundraising dinner for the basketball team. Players in his basketball program learn to work towards a goal, be part of a team, and sacrifice themselves for the common good.

In addition, the whole community benefits from the basketball team. "Our state championship last year gave everybody in Clinton something to be proud of and feel good about," Fleming said.

The basketball coach argued that people who criticize competitive sports are "barking up the wrong tree." After all, competition is part of every man and woman.

Story 8 is a press release issued by the Clinton Chamber of Commerce about the upcoming Sidewalk Festival. It contains both facts and opinions. Write an objective news story of four paragraphs, containing not more than eight sentences, using the information contained in the press release. The facts in the press release can be simply reported. The opinions should either be eliminated or else made into facts by attributing them to the Chamber of Commerce. Write your story on separate paper.

## Story 8

The most fantastic Sidewalk Festival in the history of Clinton will be held on Main Street on the weekend of June 22-24.

As usual, Main Street stores will be offering unbelievable bargains in their sidewalk displays. This year, however, the Sidewalk Festival will also include some extra-special surprises.

There will be outstanding entertainment in front of the Mr. Fix-It hardware store from 11 a.m. to 8 p.m. each day of the festival. Clinton's own favorite band, the Country Bumpkins, will kick off the festival on Friday. Also on Friday, Clintonians will have a chance to hear Laurie and the Tweeters, back by popular demand.

Both the Tweeters and the Bumpkins will be returning on Saturday and Sunday. Also performing will be an exciting new rock band, The End, and popular local folksinger Martha McKeen.

Cartoon characters much beloved by children will be visiting the Sidewalk Festival regularly. Kids will also have a great time getting their faces painted, taking a moonwalk, and watching magicians and clowns.

And if all that weren't enough, some lucky Clintonian is going to be the winner of a new color TV set. Ticket sales in the Biggest Raffle Ever begin on June 15. The drawing will be held at the grand finale of the Sidewalk Festival in front of Mr. Fix-It at 8 p.m. on June 24.

Come on, Clintonians, to the Sidewalk Festival. You won't want to miss it!

# 19. Use Modifiers Sparingly

> Kimberly Ross is a healthy, normal six-year-old girl, who plays happily with her first-grade classmates.
>
> Two years ago, Kim was wasted and wracked with pain, a victim of the most dreaded of diseases—leukemia.
>
> The reason for the gutsy little girl's miraculous recovery is one of the most incredible operations in modern medicine, a bone-marrow transplant.

The example above is the kind of writing that often appears in tabloid newspapers sold in supermarkets. Its purpose is not just to inform us about Kimberly. The writer is also trying to get us to feel sympathy for her, joy at her recovery, and admiration for the medical techniques that saved her.

Most of the words that bring out these feelings in us are modifiers—words that describe other words. Kimberly now is described as a *healthy and normal* girl who plays *happily*. Leukemia is described as a *dreaded* disease, and Kimberly is described as having been *wasted and wracked with pain*. Finally, Kimberly is described as *gutsy*, her recovery as *miraculous*, and the operation as *incredible*.

The main facts in these three paragraphs could be reported without the modifiers as follows:

> Kimberly Ross, 6, has recovered from leukemia as a result of a bone-marrow transplant operation.

Although this sentence contains the same information as the three paragraphs above, it does not have the same emotional content. As we saw in the last chapter, news stories are supposed to contain facts, not opinions or feelings. To make sure that their stories contain only facts, newswriters use very few modifiers.

Most information comes from nouns and verbs. These words provide the "cast of characters" and tell us what is happening.

## Modifiers That Are Value Words

The modifiers in the story about Kimberly Ross are value words. They tell us how we should think or feel about what is happening. There are many other examples of modifiers that are value words.

> He is being represented by a shady lawyer.
> The Tigers are counting on their outstanding halfback, Wally Dennison.
> She fought courageously to have the law changed.

There are hundreds of other modifiers that are directed towards our opinions or feelings. Some examples are: *bad, beautiful, bravely, easily, fantastic, good, lovable, sensitive, vigorously,* and *warlike.*

## Modifiers That Provide Color

Some modifiers are more neutral. They are used to provide color or detail rather than essential information.

> The owner of the company drives a large, black foreign car.

That a car is large, that it is black, and that it is foreign are all facts. Nevertheless, reporting these facts serves more to give us an impression of the owner of the company than to give us hard information about him.

The modifiers in the following sentences are also color words:

> The tall, blue-eyed candidate will be campaigning in Clinton this afternoon.
> The unshaven man haltingly told the judge that he had not been anywhere near Main Street on the night of the robbery.

**Assignment:** In Stories 1 and 2, circle the modifiers that are value or color words. The first one is done for you.

### Story 1

A (menacing) gang of undisciplined youths threatened a sweet, frail old woman on Main Street yesterday. Acting efficiently, police arrived before the youths could harm the terrified woman.

Beatrice Leluk, 78, the beloved grandmother of six cute grandchildren, was innocently doing some shopping on Main Street when one of the rascally youths came at her with a long, sharp knife. Another youth made an obscene gesture while a third spoke roughly to Mrs. Leluk.

Burly officer Ian Holt fortunately came on the scene and expertly broke up the unsavory gang.

Recovering from her frightening experience in her modest home on Chestnut Street, Mrs. Leluk said quiveringly, "Nothing like this has ever happened to me before. I don't like the way Clinton is changing."

### Story 2

Clinton fittingly honored one of its most eminent citizens yesterday in an inspiring ceremony at the Town Hall.

Lt.-Col. Donald Sterling, who had an outstanding record of service in World War II and the Korean Conflict, received the key to the Town of Clinton on his 65th birthday.

The distinguished soldier, who at 65 retains his erect posture, was visibly moved as Mayor Edward Johnson proudly declared him "an example to Clinton's youth."

Col. Sterling fought valiantly at Iwo Jima, was gravely wounded at Guadalcanal, and ably commanded a company in Korea. Since his retirement from the army, he has given valuable advice as a consultant to a number of Clinton businesses.

# Modifiers That Provide Information

Some modifiers do provide important information. Some examples are:

Number words, such as *one, five, seventeen*
Time words, such as *yesterday, now, tomorrow*
Identifying words, such as *this, that, another*

Modifiers like these are usually necessary to the sentences in which they appear.

The <u>new</u> <u>closing</u> hours for bars in Clinton go into effect <u>tomorrow</u>.

The modifiers *new, closing*, and *tomorrow* tell us something we need to know. *Closing* tells us which hours the writer is referring to. *New* tells us that the hours are being changed. *Tomorrow* tells us when this change goes into effect. The sentence would be meaningless without these modifiers:

The hours for bars in Clinton go into effect.

Similarly, consider the modifier in the following sentence:

The <u>former</u> mayor of Clinton, John Peckford, is the speaker.

If the modifier *former* were taken out, the sentence would read:

The mayor of Clinton, John Peckford, is the speaker.

Taking out the modifier distorts the meaning of the sentence. John Peckford is not the mayor of Clinton. He used to be the mayor. Now he is correctly described as the former mayor.

Modifiers that provide information are necessary in any form of writing, including newswriting. Modifiers that are value words or that only add color and detail should be avoided in newswriting. Avoid them, also, in any form of writing in which your purpose is to provide information and you wish to be objective and neutral.

**Assignment:** In Stories 3 and 4, there is a box after certain modifiers. Write an **I** in the box after the modifier if it provides essential information. Write a **V** if it is a value or color word. The first one is done for you.

**Story 3**

Police removed the reeking [V] body of a dead [ ] man from a dilapidated [ ] house on Highway 14 yesterday [ ] and took his befuddled [ ] cousin into custody.

Elmer Firth, 86, died about [ ] seven [ ] weeks ago, police reported. His cousin Alvin Firth, 82, kept the body in a lifelike [ ] position in bed until police discovered it.

Police acted when a worried [ ] neighbor reported that she had not seen either Firth for a long [ ] time. The two [ ] eccentric [ ] cousins lived like hermits but were known to emerge occasionally [ ] from the ill-kept [ ] house with peeling [ ] shutters and an overgrown [ ] yard.

Police arrived at the grisly [ ] scene at 2 p.m. yesterday. [ ] They gently [ ] questioned Alvin Firth and discovered that he believed his cousin was still [ ] alive.

After leading Alvin away, they took Elmer Firth's body to the morgue. Elmer will be buried tomorrow [ ] at 11 a.m. at Greenwood Cemetery.

Alvin Firth is undergoing psychiatric [ ] tests and is expected to be taken to a nursing [ ] home.

**Story 4**

This [ ] year's Clinton High [ ] School French [ ] Revue will feature the sunny [ ] South of France.

Performed by the 12th [ ] grade French [ ] class under the expert [ ] guidance of their teacher, Louise Parent, the revue will take the audience on a brief [ ] tour of the picturesque [ ] region.

In songs, skits, and readings, the revue will visit the colorful [ ] port of Marseilles; the fabulous [ ] French Riviera; and Arles, home of the famous [ ] painter, Vincent Van Gogh.

There will be two [ ] performances of the revue, April 24 and 25 at 8 p.m. Tickets will be available [ ] starting tomorrow [ ] in the high school administrative [ ] office.

Edit Story 5 to take out modifiers that do not give necessary information. (The marks to use in editing are shown in Instructions for Editing at the beginning of this book.) The first sentence is done for you.

## Story 5

Linda Seaborn won first prize at the annual Clinton Science Fair this weekend for her ~~ingenious~~ representation of the "Big Bang."

As the judges announced their decision in the crowded Clinton High School auditorium Sunday afternoon, the vivacious high school senior said happily, "I just can't believe it."

Seaborn is a brilliant student, who has easily achieved straight A's in all her science courses this year.

For her outstanding effort in the science fair, she will get a $250 scholarship applicable to her college tuition. She hopes to study physics at a prestigious eastern university such as Harvard or Princeton.

Cleverly constructed with billiard balls, Popsicle sticks, wire, and paint, Seaborn's model shows how scientists believe the universe began. The bewildering theory of the Big Bang says that the universe exploded from a dense ball of matter billions of years ago.

Second prize went to Jay Oland for his informative display on "Test Tube Babies." Oland has already been accepted into a challenging pre-medical course at the University of Texas.

The work of these two ambitious and talented Clinton students will be on display at Valley View Mall for the next two weeks.

# 20. Put Important Points First

Organizing your thoughts is very important when you want to make a point in writing. Organization is more important in writing than in speaking. In conversation, you can raise or lower your voice and change its tone. You can use "body language" to help make your meaning clear. Also, your listener can interrupt you if he doesn't understand. In writing, you lack these ways of making yourself clear. So you have to make your point through effective organization.

## Pyramid Style

Newswriting has its own kind of organization. In a news story, the first sentence contains the most important fact. This sentence is called the lead. The next sentence contains the second most important fact, and so on down through the story. This form of writing is often compared to an upside-down pyramid. For this reason, it is called pyramid style.

**MOST IMPORTANT**
**Second Most Important**
**third most important**
**least**
**important**

The following stories are written in pyramid style:

**Example 1:**     Arthur Norton of the state Department of Environmental Management will be the guest speaker at tomorrow's regular weekly luncheon meeting of the Clinton Rotary Club.

The meeting will begin at noon at Mike's Family Restaurant.

Mr. Norton's topic will be "Protecting Our Water Resources."

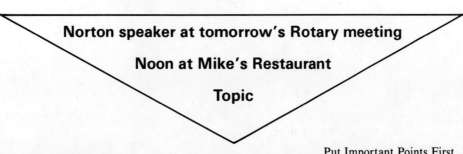

**Norton speaker at tomorrow's Rotary meeting**

**Noon at Mike's Restaurant**

**Topic**

**Example 2:**

A Clinton woman was robbed at knifepoint last night at the corner of Elm and Hill streets.

Margaret Kelly, 32, reported to police that a young male threatened her with a knife and took her pocketbook containing about $100 and credit cards.

Police are investigating the incident.

**Woman robbed at knifepoint last night.**

**Young male stole Margaret Kelly's pocketbook.**

**Police investigating.**

**Example 3:**

The Clinton library is offering summer story hours for pre-schoolers starting next Thursday.

Story hours will be held every Thursday morning at 10:30 for seven weeks.

In addition to a story read by children's librarian Paula Scrivener, each program will include crafts, games, and songs.

Pre-registration is required.

**Library story hours start next Thurs.**

**Thurs. 10:30 am for 7 weeks**

**Also crafts, games, songs**

**Pre-registration**

**Assignment:** In Story 1, the facts are arranged in order of importance. Show this by summarizing the facts in each paragraph and writing them in the pyramid at the bottom of the page in the same order as in the story.

### Story 1

Long-time Clinton resident Rose Hepburn celebrated her 90th birthday Saturday with a party at the home of her daughter, Martha Roberts of Mill Street.

Guests at the party included State Representative Elliott Woodsworth, Mayor Edward Johnson, and Rev. Charles Axworthy, in addition to Mrs. Hepburn's four daughters, 16 of her 18 grandchildren, and many of her friends.

Mrs. Hepburn taught fourth grade at Clinton Elementary School for 32 years until her retirement in 1960. Her husband, George Hepburn, died in 1971.

Rep. Woodsworth paid tribute to Mrs. Hepburn as "a wonderful influence on two generations of Clinton's youth."

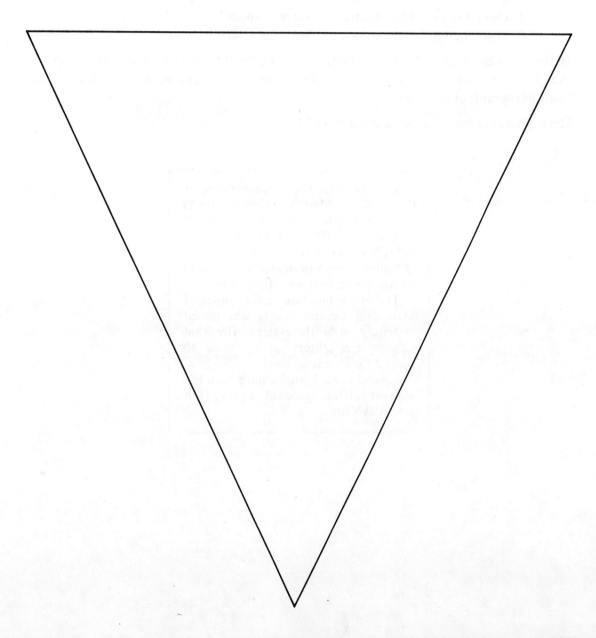

# Finding the Lead

Pyramid style is often used to make sure that a story makes its point. People often read newspapers quickly. They don't have time to read a story from beginning to end. If the most important piece of information isn't given first, people may not get to it.

Parents with young children are likely to be interested in the article about the summer story hour. Once they find out what the story is about by reading the lead, they will read on to learn the details: the time of the story hour, the content of the program, and the need for pre-registration. Someone who does not have a young child will not have to read past the first paragraph.

Similarly, in the Rotary Club story, a business person who attends Rotary Club meetings will read past the first paragraph to find out the time of the meeting and the topic of the speaker's address. Someone who does not attend Rotary Club meetings will glance quickly at the first paragraph and then go on to something else.

In deciding whether a piece of information is important enough to be used as your lead, ask yourself two questions:

1. Does it tell the reader what the story is about?
2. Does it contain new information for the reader?

In the story about Mrs. Hepburn's birthday party, the fact that she taught fourth grade may be important, but it is "old news." Thus, there is no need to mention it until the third paragraph of the story.

Here is an example of a "scrambled story":

---

Built in 1882, the office building at the corner of Main and Central streets was one of the oldest in Clinton. It housed the offices of O'Malley and O'Malley law firm, as well as the O'Malley family's insurance agency, until its conversion to town offices in 1946.

The office building at the corner of Main and Central streets was gutted yesterday in a three-alarm fire that Clinton firefighters were unable to control for almost an hour.

Several town agencies have been left without office space as a result of yesterday's fire.

---

Obviously, the fact that the building burned should come before such details as when it was built and who occupied the offices. The story is weak because it takes too long to come to the point. It would be much better if it were written as follows:

> The office building at the corner of Main and Central streets was gutted yesterday in a three-alarm fire that Clinton firefighters were unable to control for almost an hour.
>
> Several town agencies have been left without office space as a result of yesterday's fire.
>
> Built in 1882, the office building at the corner of Main and Central streets was one of the oldest in Clinton. It housed the offices of the O'Malley and O'Malley law firm, as well as the O'Malley family's insurance agency, until its conversion to town offices in 1946.

The following is another scrambled story. The sentence that should be the lead is underlined:

> Any time after December 1, a heavy snowfall may hit Clinton, forcing snow removal crews to go into action.
>
> The town council sets winter parking rules to make snow removal easier.
>
> Motorists who do not obey these rules are subject to a $50 fine.
>
> <u>Starting tomorrow, overnight parking will be forbidden on Main Street, Central Street, Elm Street and the east side of Railroad Street.</u>
>
> These rules will remain in effect until April 1.

## Unscrambling a Story

Now we will unscramble the whole story so that it is organized in pyramid style.

> Starting tomorrow, overnight parking will be forbidden on Main Street, Central Street, Elm Street and the east side of Railroad Street.
>
> These rules will remain in effect until April 1.
>
> Motorists who do not obey these rules are subject to a $50 fine.
>
> The town council sets winter parking rules to make snow removal easier.
>
> Any time after December 1, a heavy snowfall may hit Clinton, forcing snow removal crews to go into action.

**Assignment:** Stories 2 and 3 are scrambled stories. In each story, circle the sentence that should be the lead.

### Story 2

Ice hockey has been an increasingly popular sport in Clinton in recent years.

It was only three years ago that the athletics department of Clinton High School decided to start an ice hockey team and hire a hockey coach.

In its first two years, the Clinton skaters did not do very well against longer-established teams, but this season they have shown signs of improvement.

Clinton's hockey Tigers came from behind to beat the Centerville Eagles 5-3 Saturday afternoon in Centerville.

Jack Barry led the Clinton attack with two goals, including the winning goal midway through the third period.

Goaltender Eddie Frost was outstanding in the Tiger net, stopping 30 shots and holding back a determined Eagle attack in the last five minutes of the game.

### Story 3

The Recreation Department sponsors many events throughout the year for Clintonians of all ages.

The latest event announced by the department will be of interest to Clinton residents who are at least 60 years of age.

The Clinton Recreation Department will be running a senior citizens' bus trip to Washington, D.C. from October 24-29.

Included in the package are bus transportation to and from Washington, three nights' accommodation at the Harrington Hotel, and guided tours in the Washington area highlighting the White House, the Capitol, the Smithsonian Institution, and the National Gallery.

Anyone interested should contact Recreation Director Pearl Brant by telephone at 893-5627.

Unscramble Stories 4 and 5 so that they are organized in pyramid style. First, find the paragraph with the most important piece of information—your lead. Write a 1 next to it in the left-hand margin. Then find the paragraph with the next most important piece of information. Write a 2 next to it. Continue in this way to the end of the story. (There could be more than one right answer. Be prepared to say why you chose the order you did.)

### Story 4

Dr. John Nielsen has written two books on the subject of child abuse: *The Bruised Child*, which came out four years ago, and *The Hidden Problem*, which was just published this spring.

Dr. John Nielsen, who practices at City Hospital in Springfield, is recognized as one of the state's leading experts on child abuse.

A joint effort by legal authorities, the medical profession, and the community is needed to deal with child abuse, Dr. John Nielsen believes. "Child abuse is not just a problem for a few families," he wrote in his new book. "It is a problem that affects all of us."

Tomorrow evening, Dr. John Nielsen will be the guest speaker at a public lecture on child abuse sponsored by All Saints Church.

Tomorrow's lecture on child abuse will begin at 7:30 p.m. in the Social Hall in the basement of All Saints Church. The lecture is free, but contributions will be gratefully accepted.

### Story 5

Last year, Clinton received $143,758 from the state government under the State Aid to Cities and Towns Program.

Mayor Edward Johnson and other members of the town council were hoping that Clinton would receive at least as much in state aid this year as it did last year, if not more.

The notice of this year's state grant, delivered to Mayor Edward Johnson's office yesterday, came as a rude shock to the mayor.

Clinton found out yesterday that it will receive a state grant of only $96,439, almost $50,000 less than last year's grant.

"I can't understand why they would have done this," said Mayor Edward Johnson. "We're hoping it was just a mistake."

# Conversation and Newswriting

Conversation is much more loosely organized than writing is. Newspaper writers often have to write stories based on conversations they have had with people. To do this, they have to decide what information in the conversation is important to include in the story. Then they have to organize the information so that the story is in pyramid style.

Here is how an eyewitness might describe an accident:

> I was just shoveling snow when I heard a sickening crash, and I turned around, and it was my neighbor right here on Pine Street, Marjorie Welch. She had skidded on the ice and crashed into a parked car. Both cars looked like wrecks, and there was broken glass all over. It's a miracle Marjorie wasn't hurt.

A newspaper story about the same accident might read like this:

> Marjorie Welch of Pine Street was unhurt this morning when her car skidded into a parked car near her home.
>
> Both cars were extensively damaged in the collision.

**Assignment:** Reporter Lynn Drew answers the telephone in the *Clinton Daily News* office. This is the conversation that follows:

Lynn: Hello.

Caller: Hello, could I please speak to somebody in the news department?

Lynn: I'm Lynn Drew. I'm a reporter here.

Caller: Oh, hello. Isn't Ken Drew your brother? I went to high school with him. He would remember me as Lisa O'Reilly. But I'm called Sister Agatha now.

Lynn: You're a nun?

Caller: Yes. I work in India. How is Ken doing?

Lynn: Great. He lives in California now. He's a computer technician.

Caller: Yes, Ken always was one for machines. Well, the reason I'm calling is that I have a story that I thought your paper might be interested in. Have you ever heard of the wolf boy of India?

Lynn: Vaguely, but I don't know much about him.

Caller: Well, he was a boy who was found in the wild being raised by wolves about 12 years ago. We had been taking care of him in the mission where I work. I just got a letter from one of the nuns there, Sister Maria, that says he died.

Lynn: I'm sorry to hear that. What did he die of?

Caller: No one seems to know. He was fine when I left about six months ago. I'm taking a year to study in the United States and I'm just visiting family in Clinton. But it seems he just got sick, and nothing the doctors could do helped him.

Lynn: Could you tell me more about him?

Caller: Well, we didn't really know much about him because he never learned to talk. He just made sounds like an animal. He did learn to dress himself, although it wasn't easy to teach him. And he learned to bathe. When he was found, his hair was all matted. He also learned to walk like a man, although he sometimes liked to walk on all fours, the way he did when they found him playing with wolf cubs.

Lynn: How old was he?

Caller: Well, we don't know exactly, of course, but we think he was about 10 when he was found, so he must have been about 22.

Lynn: Well, thank you very much for calling. I'm going to write a story about the wolf boy right now.

Caller: Thank you. And please give my regards to Ken.

Pretend you are Lynn Drew, and write a five-paragraph news story based on your conversation with Sister Agatha. To do this, find the most important piece of information about the wolf boy. Write a one-sentence paragraph in news style containing that information. That will be your lead.

Then find the next most important piece of information, and write another paragraph of one or two sentences containing that information. That will be your second paragraph.

Continue in this way until the end of the story. Don't include any information that has nothing to do with the wolf boy. Write your story on separate paper.